ANN THE WORD

BOOKS BY NARDI REEDER CAMPION

PATRICK HENRY *Firebrand of the Revolution*

KIT CARSON *Pathfinder of the West*

CASA MEANS HOME
  With Colonel Red Reeder

THE WEST POINT STORY

BRINGING UP THE BRASS *The Life of
  Sergeant Marty Maher of West Point*
  With Rosamond Wilfley Stanton

LOOK TO THIS DAY! *The Lively Education of a
  Great Woman Doctor: Connie Guion, M.D.*

ANN THE WORD: *The Life of Mother Ann Lee,
  Founder of the Shakers*

ANN THE WORD

The Life of Mother Ann Lee,
Founder of the Shakers

NARDI REEDER CAMPION

Little, Brown and Company — Boston-Toronto

FIRST EDITION

T 09/76

LIBRARY OF CONGRESS CATALOGING IN PUBLICATION DATA

Campion, Nardi Reeder.
Ann the Word.

Bibliography: p.
Includes index.
1. Lee, Ann, 1736–1784. 2. Shakers — History.
I. Title.
BX97993.L4C35   289.8′092′4 [B]   76–6568
ISBN 0–316–12767–1

Designed by Susan Windheim

Published simultaneously in Canada
by Little, Brown & Company (Canada) Limited

PRINTED IN THE UNITED STATES OF AMERICA

For

My daughter
    Narcissa Reeder Campion

My daughters-in-law
    Lynn Hillyard Campion
    Anne Daignault Campion
    Anita Montero Campion
Four independent, intelligent, invincible young women who are for me — along with Mother Ann — "morning stars of the women's movement."

"The inner life is twofold, embracing repentance—confessing and forsaking all sin—and regeneration—living according to the teachings and practice of Jesus Christ."

—*From the Doctrine of the American Society of Shakers*

"Happy are those who dream dreams and are ready to pay the price to make them come true."

—His Eminence Leon-Joseph, Cardinal Suenens

'Tis a Gift to Be Simple

'Tis a gift to be simple, 'tis a gift to be free,
'Tis a gift to come down where you ought to be,
And when we find ourselves in the place just right,
'Twill be in the valley of love and delight.
When true simplicity is gained,
To bow and to bend we shan't be ashamed.
To turn, turn will be our delight
'Till by turning, turning we come round right.

Shaker Dance Song

Chapters

Foreword

FEW EPISODES IN ALL HISTORY ARE SO COLORFUL OR
so strange as the rise of the Shakers. The United
Society of Believers in Christ's Second Appearing,
as they were originally called, was an ecstatic and
highly disciplined religious sect which evolved from
the powerful personality of an obscure, illiterate
woman named Ann Lee. The devout Shakers believed she was the female embodiment of Christ —
Ann, the Word of God made manifest.

Mother Ann, who lived only forty-eight years
(1736–1784), eventually became the spiritual
leader of thousands, and she was far more influential
than better-known Colonial heroines such as Martha
Washington, Betsy Ross, or Molly Pitcher. Ann's
dream for humanity exceeded all patriotic bound-
aries. What she did, with incredible boldness, was
to attempt to chart the most difficult of all worlds

to enter — the world of the spirit. In the process, Mother Ann founded one of the most successful experiments in communal living the world has ever known.

A wealth of material has been written about Shakerism. The three most important books are: *The Testimony of Christ's Second Appearing* by Benjamin S. Youngs (1808); *A Summary View of the Millennial Church* by Calvin Green and Seth Y. Wells (1823); and *Testimonies Concerning the Character and Ministry of Mother Ann Lee and the First Witnesses of the Gospel of Christ's Second Appearing; Given by Some of the Aged Brethren and Sisters of the United Society* (1827). These books are the most authentic records in existence of the remarkable life of Mother Ann. They are hardly impartial, being compiled by her followers, yet they give us our clearest picture of Ann Lee drawn by her contemporaries. It is a picture of a strong woman who triumphed over incredible odds to establish a society where, for a time, men and women were able to escape from the chains of competition, materialism, and self-gratification and live their lives according to Saint Paul's words in the Book of Acts: "All that believed were together, and had all things common . . and were of one heart, and of one soul."

N.R.C.

xiv

ANN THE WORD

1

Ann Lee of Toad Lane

How little can the rich man know
  Of what the poor man feels,
When Want, like some dark demon foe,
  Nearer and nearer steals!

He never saw his darlings lie
  Shivering, the grass their bed;
He never heard that maddening cry,
  Daddy, a bit of bread!
                    —Old Manchester Song

IN 1736, ON FEBRUARY 29, THAT MYSTERIOUS CALEN-
dar day that surfaces only once in four years — a
daughter was born to John Lees and his wife in their
dingy lodging on Toad Lane in the oldest quarter of
Manchester, England. The baby was named Ann,
and at her birth there was nothing to indicate her remarkable destiny; yet this baby girl, Ann Lee of
Toad Lane, would one day have thousands of devout
followers who thought of her as the Female Christ.

In *Testimonies Concerning the Character and
Ministry of Mother Ann Lee,* the book of rem-
iniscences about Ann collected from people who
knew her, Ann's parents are described as poor but
honest laborers. Her father, John Lees (the *s* was

later dropped) was a blacksmith who had to work as a tailor at night to eke out a meager living for his family. He was "respectable in character, moral in principle, honest and punctual in his dealings, and industrious in business." Her mother was "esteemed as a strictly religious and very pious woman." As often happened in those days, the mother's name was not even recorded.

Of Ann's youth, little is known. She was the second of the Lees' eight children. The registry of Christ Church in Manchester documents Ann Lee's private baptism on June 1, 1742, when she was six years old. It also notes the baptisms of several of her seven brothers and sisters, but aside from this nothing of the early years has come to light.

But of Ann's early surroundings, a great deal is known. Manchester, a black, sprawling city in the center of England, was a place most people preferred to think did not exist. It was a disgrace. The wealth of its textile mills was built on degradation and poverty. The laborers lived close to the mills in unspeakable squalor, while the mill owners lived out in the country, the windows of their elegant Georgian homes facing the rolling green meadows and beautiful woods of Lancashire. The owners allowed themselves to see as little as possible of the workers' misery.

Along with the other children in that godforsaken city, Ann Lee went to work in the mills when she

A view of Toad Lane.

A view of eighteenth-century Manchester.

was eight years old. There was no question of going to school; the opportunity simply did not exist. Ann did not learn to read or write then, or ever. Like most intelligent illiterates, she developed a strong memory and, in later life, her knowledge of the Bible was prodigious.

In *Testimonies* she is described as an attractive girl, short and somewhat plump, with light chestnut-brown hair, blue eyes, and fair complexion. We are told she was neat, thoughtful, hard-working, and "never addicted to play like other children," as though play were some kind of weakness. In eighteenth-century Manchester, childhood was a blight to be overcome as soon as possible.

Young Ann's first job was as a cutter of velvet. Later she prepared cotton for the looms and sheared fur for the hat makers. She worked twelve hours a day, on her feet the entire time because no seats were provided for children. On Sundays, like the other children, she helped clean the equipment, hoping not to be injured by the dangerous machinery.

The mill owners apparently suffered not the slightest twinge of conscience from their exploitation of child labor. Robert Southey, the poet laureate of England who visited Manchester in 1808, said the mill supervisor claimed that infinite good resulted from putting little children to work. " 'You see these children, sir,' said he. 'They get their

bread almost as soon as they can walk about, and by
the time they are seven or eight years old bring in
money. There is no idleness amongst us; they come
at five in the morning, we allow them half an hour
for breakfast and an hour for dinner; they leave
work at six and another set relieves them for the
night; the wheels never stand still.' "

Growing up in Manchester must have been a
nightmare for a girl who was as sensitive as Ann Lee.
The weather varied from misty to damp to rainy; the
houses were overcrowded and dirty; the streets
reeked with animal and human excrement. The
only escape available to the workers from their appalling living conditions was drinking, and there was
plenty of that. Beer houses and gin mills, competing
for the laborer's money, opened at the earliest hour
and stayed open most of the night. One observer
wrote, "It is not just adult males who come to the
taverns to drug their minds with alcohol. Alas, no.
The mother with her wailing baby, the young girl
with her sweetheart, the half-clad, ill-fed child — all
are jumbled together in those dirty dens of drink."

It is easy to understand how Ann, repelled by the
evils around her, developed a habit of retreating into
the world of her imagination. "She was a very peculiar child from infancy," wrote Aurelia Mace, in her
early Shaker history *The Aletheia*, "and often told of
having visions of supernatural things." This vivid

imagination was to play an important part in Ann's future life.

The children of Manchester were spared no details of life, death, or procreation. Like all the others, Ann used the open toilets with the adults and shared the bedroom with her parents. Perhaps this is why, as a young girl, she developed a strong antipathy toward sex. *Testimonies* gives a dramatic picture of Ann's efforts to prevent her mother from having intercourse with her father.

> In early youth Ann Lee had a great abhorrence of the fleshly cohabitation of the sexes, and so great was her sense of its impurity, that she often admonished her mother against it, which, coming to her father's ears, he threatened and actually attempted to whip her; upon which she threw herself into her mother's arms and clung around her neck to escape his strokes.

Ann Lee's mother, described as "a good woman, able to instruct and guide her," died early. Ann was left to bring up the younger children. She did her best to teach them right from wrong but it was almost impossible to combat the moral decay of Manchester. She herself might easily have given up and embraced the animal-like existence of the mill workers, had she not found an unexpected source of strength. Ann discovered religion.

The established church, which she had joined as a child, was utterly meaningless to her. The coldly intellectual Church of England was more concerned with ritual and power than with the plight of the common people who were at the mercy of brutal laws. (The American Sam Adams called it "the whore of Babylon.") In those days, two hundred and fifty-three offenses were punishable by death. A man could be hanged if he shot a rabbit, cut down a tree, or stole five shillings' worth of property. Even a ten-year-old could be sentenced to death. Ann Lee was revolted by a church that could ignore these conditions.

About this time two powerful religious figures appeared on the horizon, the great English preachers John Wesley and George Whitefield. Through unceasing effort, this pair of zealous evangelists revived personal religion in England. Because they conducted their worship by "rule and method," they were called Methodists. In the face of continuous insults and persecution, they passionately preached the Gospel and aroused the workers to awareness of their rights as children of God.

When the Reverend George Whitefield came to Manchester to preach there was great excitement. Ann Lee, eager to hear the famous man, joined the throng that crowded around his outdoor pulpit. Because the disapproving Anglican Church closed its doors to him, Whitefield held his revival meetings under the trees. What he had to say about the all-powerful love of God was not new, but his inflammatory preaching and his outdoor church were. In glowing terms Whitefield described the direct influence the Holy Spirit could have on a person's daily life. Ann was deeply affected by his eloquence and by the crowd's emotional, almost hysterical, response. Whitefield showed her the great power an electrifying preacher could generate. It was a lesson Ann Lee never forgot.

As she struggled to find some meaning in her dreary existence, Ann became increasingly absorbed in the worship of God. It was the year 1758 that marked the turning point in her life. Just twenty-two, and working as a cook in the Manchester infirmary (which was also a "lunatic hospital") to escape from the mills, Ann attended a series of religious revival meetings lead by Jane and James Wardley. From that time on, her life began to change, at first gradually and then dramatically.

The Wardleys were poor tailors from a town near Manchester called Bolton-on-the-Moors. Originally they had been devout Quakers, dedicated to the belief that true religion comes from inward experience. But in 1747, they received a spiritual message — "a further degree of light and power" — that led them to separate from the Society of Friends and form their own more emotional group called the Wardley Society. They developed an expressive kind of worship that seemed to transport people from the suffering and sorrows of the physical world to an exalted plane in the spiritual world. The Wardleys were strongly influenced by the ecstatic worship of a radical French group, called Camisards, who migrated to Lancashire in 1658 after Protestantism was forbidden in France.

Ann Lee was filled with enthusiasm for the new movement and she soon joined the Wardley Society. She found their meetings deeply satisfying. The services would begin in true Quaker fashion with men and women sitting in silent meditation. Then they would rise, one by one, and confess their sins. Ann was affected by what she heard. Was it possible that her sins, too, might be redeemed by repentance and confession? She had long been suffocated by an overpowering sense of sin, because she was unable to meet the total demands of the Christian faith. "Many times when I was about my work," she said later, "I felt my soul overwhelmed with sorrow and I would work as long as I could to keep it concealed, and then run to get out of sight, lest some one should pity me with that pity which God did not."

In addition to open confession, the Wardley services included impassioned preaching, usually by Mother Jane. In glowing words, she would describe the new era that was coming and tell of mystical experiences — heavenly voices, lights in the sky, and visions. She riveted the congregation, not only by her apocalyptic eloquence, but by the simple fact she was a woman. A female preacher was unheard of in Manchester, England.

The climax of the meetings came when the worshippers were moved to express their inner feelings in physical terms. They would start by walking the floor, chanting and singing. Soon they would be shouting, shaking, and dancing. Because of this they were called "Shaking Quakers," a name first used in ridicule but later widely accepted.

Jane and James Wardley became invaluable to Ann. In them she found parental figures who offered the firm moral and spiritual guidance she had yearned for. Their meetings gave her life new meaning. The cleansing power of repentance and the acting out of sinful feelings were vital, but there was another facet of the movement that held a strong attraction for her. It was a revolutionary idea, blasphemous some said. Even today, it would be considered radical. In eighteenth-century England, it was unthinkable. The Shaking Quakers believed that Christ was coming again to reign on earth — and that His second appearance would be in the form of a woman.

Ann Lee watched Mother Jane lead the meetings, eloquently proclaiming her belief that God was both male and female, that Christ represented the male principle but the female principle was yet to come. Ann listened intently as she read from Jeremiah: "How long wilt thou go about, O thou backsliding daughter? For the Lord hath created a new thing in the earth, a woman shall compass a man." And Ann Lee wondered, could it be true? *Was it possible the kingdom of God really would be brought forth on earth by a woman?*

2

Marriage and Misery

Wives, submit yourselves to your own
husbands, as unto the Lord. For the
husband is the head of the wife, even as
Christ is the head of the church. . . .
Therefore, as the church is subject unto
Christ, so let the wives be to their husbands
in everything.
> —SAINT PAUL in the Epistle to the
> Ephesians, Chapter 5, verses 22–25.

IN ANN LEE'S DAY, WOMEN WERE POSSESSIONS. THEY were the playthings, the ornaments, or the servants of men. A few, a very few, managed to achieve their independence. Ann Lee was one of these.

In eighteenth-century England, the intelligence of women was held in low esteem. Lord Chesterfield, that urbane man of letters, was probably speaking for most of his countrymen when he said, "Women are to be talked to as below men and above children." Women had no legal existence apart from their husbands. They could not vote, sign contracts, or own property. Married women had no title to their own earnings or even, in the event of legal separation, to their own children. Few women went to school and none went to the universities. It was accepted as a fact that a woman was not capable of taking care of herself. If she had no husband, her father or brothers were responsible for her.

Because Ann Lee's father considered marriage essential to his daughter's security, he insisted that she had to marry whether she wanted to or not. Ann was twenty-six years old and the revulsion against sex, which she had expressed so openly in childhood, still plagued her, but her father gave her no choice. He not only compelled her to marry, he even selected her husband, his own hard-working apprentice Abraham Standerin (later called Stanley).

Ann Lee may now be considered a morning star of the women's movement, but at that time she was meekly obedient to her father's commands. Hence it was that on Tuesday, January 5, 1762, "Ann Lees, spinster," was married to "Abraham Standerin, blacksmith." Although Ann had belonged to the Wardley's Shaking Quakers for four years, she was married in her father's Anglican church. Because both the bride and the groom were illiterate, they signed the marriage register with x's. Then they moved in with Ann's father.

The legal concept that marriage creates one person, and at the expense of the woman, was established by William Blackstone, the great English jurist who lived at the same time as Ann Lee. Black-

Banns of Marriage _Abraham Standerin and Ann Lees were_
Published on Sunday Dec.r 20.th 27.th and January 3.d 1762 the said
Abraham Standerin – of _this_ Parish _and Town of Manchester_

N°
7
Blacksmith — and _Ann Lees_ of _this_
Parish _and Town of Manchester_ _Spinster_ were
Married in this _Church_ by _Banns_ this
fifth Day of _January_ in the Year One Thousand Seven
Hundred and _Sixty One_ by me. _Maurice Griffith_

This Marriage was solemnized between Us { _abraham_ × _Standerin:_ mark
ann × _Lees:_ mark

In the Prefence of _James Shethird_
Tho.s Hulme

The bans of marriage between Abraham Standerin and Ann
Lees.

stone stated flatly: "The very being or legal existence
of the woman is suspended during marriage, or at
least incorporated and consolidated into that of the
husband." But Ann refused to go along with that
idea. Showing a remarkable independence of spirit,
she continued to be known as Ann Lee, not Ann
Stanley.

Ann's husband was a lusty, good-humored fellow,
"kind according to nature," who did not understand
his complicated, emotional wife. It would be hard
to imagine two people who were more different.
Ann, we are told, yearned for a higher life and was
always looking for "someone to assist her in the
pursuit of true holiness"; while Abraham Stanley is
described as "a decent man who liked his beef and
his beer, his corner by the fireplace, and his chair
at the tavern."

According to *Testimonies*, these two "lived

16

together at her father's house, in peace and harmony, and procured a comfortable living." But this must be a rosy overstatement because the word "peace" simply does not fit the facts. The marriage of Ann and Abraham was stalked by tragedy from the beginning.

It was normal for an eighteenth-century wife to be continuously pregnant and Ann was no exception. She gave birth to four children in rapid succession. All of her deliveries were difficult and forceps had to be used in the last one, leaving Ann "lying for hours with little appearance of life." Although she was naturally maternal, the rearing of children was not to be her role. Three of her children died when they were babies and the fourth, Elizabeth, died at the age of six. The Cathedral registry records the burial on October 7, 1766, of "Elizabeth, daughter of Abraham Stanley." The mother's name is not important enough to mention.

The deaths of her four children left Ann Lee almost paralyzed by grief and guilt. She had what would now be called a complete nervous breakdown. Her traumatic suffering is described in A Summary View of the Millennial Church, that first Shaker history: "The convictions of her youth often returned upon her with great force . . . She sought deliverance from the bondage of sin, and gave herself no rest, day or night, but often spent whole nights in laboring and crying to God for deliverance from sin."

Night after night, Ann walked the floor in her

stocking feet, asking God's help. "Sometimes I went to bed and slept," she said, "but in the morning I could not feel that sense of the word of God which I did before I slept. This brought me great tribulation. Then I cried to God, and promised him, that if he would give me the same sense that I had before I slept, I would labor all night. This I did many nights." Her groans and cries far into the night made the family tremble, and once her agitation was so great that the bed rocked violently and her husband "was glad to leave it."

Surely Ann knew many women who had to bury their children; *half* the children in Manchester's working class died before the age of five. Ignoring that horrible fact, Ann Lee tried to find an explanation for her sorrow in her own behavior. As she prayed and mourned, she gradually became convinced that her unbearable tragedies were God's judgment upon her for permitting her father and Abraham Stanley to persuade her to forsake her true feelings and marry.

Now, more than ever, Ann was appalled by what she called "the great depravity of human nature and the odiousness of sin, especially of the impure and indecent nature of sexual coition." The deaths of her four children convinced her that sex and marriage were the root of all evil, as indeed they must have been to her. She announced her conclusion to all who would listen: sexual sin had caused her catastrophes.

In desperation she turned to the Wardleys for help. We have in Ann's own words a description of her despair and Mother Jane's peculiar solution for her crisis: "I fell under heavy trials and tribulation on account of lodging with my husband and as I looked to the Wardleys for help and counsel, I opened my trials to Jane. She said, 'James and I lodge together but we do not touch each other any more than two babes. You may return and do likewise.'"

What a relief those words must have been to a woman in hysterical torment. Simply by following the instructions of her spiritual advisor, Ann could escape sexual intercourse, which she loathed, and the inevitable pregnancies as well. She adopted Mother Jane's formula literally. To keep from stirring up her husband's affections, Ann avoided their bed "as if it had been made of embers." She said that she denied herself "every gratification of a carnal nature" and was even afraid to close her eyes at night lest she "awake in hell."

And how did Abraham Stanley take his wife's sudden conversion to celibacy? Not quietly. He was deeply devoted to his zealous wife and her departure from his bed infuriated him. He had violent arguments with her, as all their neighbors could testify. When those proved fruitless, he marched over to the cathedral and angrily complained to the clergy of his wife's conduct. The priests tried to help him. They confronted Ann with the Bible, quoting Saint Paul's directive to women: *Wives, submit yourselves to your own husbands, as unto the Lord.* It was to no avail. Ann was adamant. She was now certain that only a total denial of the body could purify her tortured soul. She would never again have sexual relations with her husband. That was final.

The amazing thing is that Abraham Stanley did not leave his wife. Coping with a preaching, praying, celibate wife required more insight than one would expect from a blacksmith who couldn't write his own name, yet he remained faithful. Indeed, his devotion to her seemed to increase. Ann is quoted as saying, "He would have been willing to pass through a flaming fire for my sake, if I would only live in the flesh with him, which I refused to do." Instead of departing, Abraham Stanley surprised everybody, perhaps even himself. He decided that he, too, would join the Shaking Quakers.

Her husband's conversion to Shakerism and to celibacy is the earliest proof we have of the power of Ann Lee's personality.

3

She Preachers

Sir, a woman's preaching is like a
dog's walking on his hind legs. It
is not done well, but you are surprised
to find it done at all.
— DR. SAMUEL JOHNSON (1709–1784)

MOTHER JANE WARDLEY WAS A PROPHET "FILLED with the Holy Spirit" who could enflame a crowd with her passionate preaching. "Amend your lives!" Mother Jane cried. "Repent, for the Kingdom of God is at hand!" And Ann Lee responded with all her heart and soul. Ann, who never did anything halfway, was by now a dedicated celibate, deeply immersed in the Wardley movement and looking to Mother Jane for her soul's salvation.

The fact that a woman was preaching at all inspired Ann Lee. Many forces in eighteenth-century England kept women repressed, but none was more powerful than the church, where Saint Paul's letter to the Corinthians was used — as it is even today —

to define a woman's place: *Let your women keep silence in the churches: for it is not permitted unto them to speak . . . And if they will learn any thing, let them ask their husbands at home: for it is a shame for women to speak in church.*

The revolutionary idea that a woman might actually be allowed to preach seems to have originated with the Quakers. George Fox, founder of the Society of Friends, was not a feminist *per se*, but he believed that the spirit of God resides within every human being and must be listened to. Under Fox's direction, Quaker women were given positions of leadership as early as 1670. Some of his followers, however, considered the idea so monstrous that they left the Society in protest.

The Wardleys wholeheartedly adopted the Quakers' radical acceptance of women. They encouraged women to speak and Ann Lee, who was to become one of the most effective women preachers of all time, did her first public speaking when she stood up and confessed at their meetings. Confession, that "cleansing river" as it is called in the fifteenth-century morality play *Everyman*, was the wellspring of the Wardley revivals. Mother Jane told Ann she would never reach God unless she could confess her sins and get rid of everything within her that was not "of God." Of course, Mother Jane added, repentance must go hand in hand with confession; without it, confession was of no value whatsoever.

Repentance came easily to Ann; confession did not. True, she had grown up in the Anglican Church which, like the Roman Catholic Church, considered private confession between parishioner and priest invaluable for anyone struggling to lead a Christian life. But the Wardleys demanded "open confession of every known sin" — an altogether different situation.

Ann Lee began her public confessions hesitantly, but before long she was pouring out her transgressions. What a welcome release this must have been for a woman riddled with self-inflicted guilt after the deaths of all her children. She threw herself into an emotional account of her "manifold sins and wickednesses" and people listened, spellbound. "When I confessed my sins," she said later, "I labored to remember the time when and the place where I committed them. And when I had confessed them, I cried to God to know if my confession was accepted; and by crying to God continually I traveled out of my loss."

Thanks to modern psychiatry, we now know a great deal about the healing power of unburdening the heart. But it was two hundred years before Viennese doctors developed the "talking cure" that Ann Lee's torrent of intense confession helped her to

23

"travel out of" her loss toward a new life. As the psychologist and philosopher William James was to explain two centuries later: "For him who confesses, shams are over and realities have begun; he has exteriorized his rottenness."

It was not only impassioned confessions that helped Ann. The Wardley's insistence that their followers give physical expression to their inner turmoil was also therapeutic. During worship some people would enter into trancelike states; others, seeking release from the weight of their sins, would be overcome by twitching, shaking, and jerking. Ann joined in these strange rituals with fervor.

Under the guidance of the Wardleys, Ann Lee's new life began. Early Shaker history speaks of Jane and James Wardley as having "great power over sin" and goes on to say: "By her faithful obedience to her leaders, Ann Lee was baptized into the same spirit, and, by degrees, attained full knowledge and experience in spiritual things." It was not long before Ann, recognized as a strong spokesman for the Wardley Society, was leading meetings herself.

That Ann had an incredible talent for communicating her convictions to others is clear. She persuaded her father, her sister, two of her brothers, and as we have already seen, her husband, to join the Shaking Quakers. For downtrodden people pinched by poverty and hard work, this ecstatic religious movement must have offered new and joyous hope.

24

As Ann's personal following increased, so did her persecution by the local authorities. They considered her odd, noisy meetings a threat to the established order of the town. Time and again Ann was insulted and chased from the streets; any pretext sufficed to get this erratic woman out of the way.

One Sunday morning, Ann and her followers met in her father's house to worship as usual. Spies, who had been placed in the streets by the authorities, sounded the alarm, and a mob quickly surrounded the Lee house. With the warden leading the way, the crowd burst into the room where services were being held. In a rush of violence the worshippers were seized, dragged outside, and carted off to Manchester's stone prison, a place of horror called "The Dungeons," where prisoners faced brutality, filth, and cruel neglect. Everyone was released next morning except Ann Lee and her father, who were kept in jail several weeks for "profaning the Sabbath."

Abuse did not dishearten Ann; far from it. The more she was mistreated, the more intense her soul-searching became and the stronger her religious conviction grew. She intended to preach the Gospel and to help others find God, as she was beginning to find him, and nothing was going to stop her.

Unfortunately, detailed documentation of Ann's life in England is scant. No one knew that this obscure, poverty-stricken, unpredictable young woman would one day start an influential religious movement, and few records were kept of her early activities. As to time sequence, we do know for a fact that Ann was twenty-two years old when she joined the Wardley movement, and twenty-six when she married, but it was not until she reached the age of thirty-four that her crusade really began.

Ann Lee endured nine years of soul-searching and suffering before she felt prepared to assume her life's work. During those years, we are told, she sought God ceaselessly in "watchings, fastings, tears, and incessant prayer." At times her agony was excruciating. *Testimonies*, comparing her trials to those of Jesus when he was tempted by the Devil in the wilderness, states: "She labored, day and night, for deliverance from the very nature of sin. And under the most severe tribulation of mind, and the most violent temptations and buffetings of the enemy, she was often in such extreme agony of soul as caused the blood to perspire through the pores of her skin . . . Sometimes for whole nights together, her cries, screeches and groans were such as to fill every soul around her with fear and trembling."

The years of anguish and fasting caused Ann to waste away until she became a mere skeleton. Elder John Hocknell, a member of the Wardley Society who was with her through much of her suffering, testified that after a series of spiritual crises she was incapable of helping herself. Her naturally strong, healthy body became so emaciated that she was as weak as an infant and had to be fed and supported by others.

But occasionally during her long ordeal, much to the awe of her companions, Ann would be miraculously restored to health. It was said her face would then acquire an unearthly beauty and her eyes would glow. During these strange intervals, she resumed her preaching. Her suffering seemed to give her new power and people gathered about her, fascinated. She exhorted and coaxed until many of them made open confession. Some delivered themselves so completely of their sins they would begin to shiver and shake.

"Shake away the past!" Ann shouted. "Don the white cloaks of a new life!" Such hysterical scenes were too much for official Manchester. Again, Ann Lee was arrested and sent to the stone prison by the Irwell River. This time she was charged with "disturbing the peace."

This extraordinary woman met her trials and tribulations with calm acceptance because she believed pain was necessary to the process of coming out of herself into a broader knowledge of God's presence. In the words of the Shaker hymn, Ann Lee was convinced that in order to be saved, "We must fall on the rock and be broken."

4

A Woman Clothed With The Sun

And there appeared a great wonder
in heaven; a woman clothed with the
sun, and the moon under her feet,
and upon her head a crown of twelve
stars.

—*Revelations*, Chapter 12, Verse 1

SOME WHO HAVE EXPERIENCED RELIGIOUS CONVER-
sion say the breakthrough into a higher realm of
power brings a feeling of littleness and helplessness;
then a "holy necessity" takes over; new solutions and
new patterns are found, and life assumes a new
meaning.

This is exactly what happened to Ann Lee while
she was in prison. She was thirty-four years old, in
the year 1770, when she beheld the vision that
marked the birth of Shakerism. She had been seeking
God for nine long years but still felt "hedged up on
every side." Once more she "cried mightily to God
for help." This time her prayers were answered by
a blinding apparition.

We know that as a child Ann, like Joan of Arc, had seen visions and heard voices, but her experience in prison was of a different magnitude. According to *A Summary View*, "The most astonishing visions and divine manifestations were presented to her in so clear and striking a manner, that the whole spiritual world seemed displayed before her." In those soul-splitting moments, Ann felt that the cause of all suffering and the mystery of all evil were revealed to her. In one "glorious klang of being" she grasped the meaning of life, and felt herself resonant as a bell.

First she saw Adam and Eve in the Garden of Eden. She watched them defy God and commit the forbidden sexual act. Then she witnessed their expulsion from the garden by an enraged Deity. All at once it became crystal clear to Ann Lee there was one single cause for humanity's separation from God: *sex*. All her earlier suspicions were confirmed. It was obvious to her that all the evil in the world sprang from the hotbed of sexual desire. She realized there was only one way for humanity to recover from its lost state. To enter a new age of spirituality, men and women would have to abstain from "all lustful gratification of the flesh." Self-denial by celibacy was the first essential for those who wanted to gain the spiritual strength to reach God. This was the vision Ann Lee would carry in her heart the rest of her days.

During those moments of mystical ecstasy, a strong

current vibrated up and down her spine. Then, as all emotion drained away, a sense of release swept over her and her whole being was suffused with inner harmony and peace. She felt that all her sins were forgiven, all her problems solved. No wonder Ann Lee walked out of that dank prison filled with new power. For her the years of seeking were over. She was convinced she had found the truth, and the truth had set her free. She felt at one with God.

Skeptics say a mystic is a person who cannot cope with the real world and, therefore, flees to one of make-believe. Yet few people would deny that altered states of consciousness do occur. At every time in history and every place on the globe overwhelming, indescribable, mind-changing experiences have been recorded. Joan of Arc, Buddha, Saint Paul, Jesus, Mohammed, Thomas Aquinas, all were transported by religious ecstasy, limitless and unbounded. Ecstasy ("the lifting out of self beyond all reason and control") brought each of them rebirth, followed by an afterflow of peace and certainty that lasted a lifetime. So it was for Ann Lee, too. No one can account for these experiences. It is impossible to explain the inexplicable.

As soon as Ann was released from jail, she "took up her cross against the carnal gratifications of the flesh." Speaking with fresh eloquence, she described her vision of the Garden of Eden and attacked sex as the source and foundation of all corruption. According to Shaker historians, her exhortations were delivered with "a heart-searching and soul-quickening spirit that seemed to penetrate every secret of the heart."

She told her listeners that if they would utterly surrender their wills to God, all their earth-born lusts would die away and they would know the bliss of Divine intercourse. Transported by her vision, Ann had escaped from all demands of the flesh and found satisfaction in the world of the spirit.

This reborn woman, radiating spiritual strength, dazzled James and Jane Wardley. They proclaimed her the head of their society and news of the intense, eloquent leader spread rapidly. Simple country folk, yearning for a kinder, better life, turned to Ann for help. Factory workers, starved for hope, suddenly found their drab lives brightened by her incandescent glow.

Intensity itself can be experienced as the sign of a higher, value-filled existence. For these poor people, mired in misery, Ann's exuberance had great power. When she told them they would never know peace until they gave up sex and sought God, they believed her and expected her to lead them to their Savior.

Why should celibacy appear to Ann Lee the solution for all the ills of the world? Surely this is a key question in her life. Perhaps the deaths of her four babies left Ann with a pathological fear of pregnancy that made her reject sex. Or she may have been permanently scarred in early childhod by fear of sex. We have already seen how, as a little girl, Ann begged her mother to stay away from her father's bed. Given the lack of privacy in Toad Lane, Ann's first impressions of sexual intercourse may have been terrifying. Psychologists say that little children are apt to interpret what they see, hear, or imagine occurring between their parents in bed on the level of their own aggressive impulses. Deep in Ann's unconscious, a childish fantasy may have persisted that sex is a brutal assault by a man upon a woman.

Whatever the cause, the result is clear. In her vision, Ann received "a great light concerning the depravity of human nature." She was now convinced that "weakness of the flesh" caused all worldly sins: vanity, sloth, vulgarity, jealousy, disorder, dishonesty, greed. She knew her message was not for everyone. Of course the world's people would go on marrying and begetting children. But those who yearned for true holiness would have to follow the path of sexual purity.

Despite Ann's feeling that her problems were solved, they were actually proliferating. Her biggest difficulty still lay with the forces of law and order in Manchester. The more she called upon her followers to shun sexual relationships and purify their lives by open confession of their sins, the more sensational her meetings became. As *A Summary View* states in rather guarded language: "The most hidden abominations were often brought to light, and those secret acts of wickedness, which had been deceitfully covered under . . . were many times brought to view in such a manner as to make every guilty soul fear and tremble."

These lurid revelations of guilt attracted curious crowds who taunted and jeered at the self-proclaimed sinners. As usual, the authorities were quick to take action. An entry in the Manchester town records shows that on July 14, 1772, Ann Lee, her father (who by now was, apparently, under his daughter's spell), and two others were arrested for creating a public nuisance. They were arraigned before Justice Peter Mainwaring, who conducted hearings at the Mule Inn, where " considerable ale drinking accompanied the proceedings." At the next session of the court, blacksmith John Lee and his daughter, Ann, were sentenced to a month in prison.

Repeated sentences did nothing to dim the religious fervor now rampant in the Lee family. Three months later, the constable again broke into their Toad Lane house to quell another noisy revival meeting and, the official record states, "apprehend the gang." This time everyone present was fined, and Ann's brother, James, was carted off to jail.

It is easy to understand why the local authorities

considered the Shakers, as they were now called, a threat to the establishment. Shaker membership was increasing and so was Shaker vehemence against the Church of England. Under Ann Lee's leadership, they repeatedly attacked the church for indifference to the suffering of its people and for "condoning marriage." *The Manchester Mercury* of July 20, 1773, reported that Ann, her sister Betty, and two men marched into Christ Church in Manchester and there willfully and contemptuously, in the time of Divine service, disturbed the congregation then assembled at morning prayers. This was an act of almost unbelievable daring, especially for two women, and the authorities were shocked. Again, all were arrested. This time they were fined the staggering sum of twenty pounds. Since they could never raise that amount of money, once more they were packed off to prison. Nothing daunted, as soon as Ann got out she resumed her inflammatory preaching. There was no limit to her determination to share God's truth.

The word *fanatic* comes from the Latin *fanaticus*, which means "to be put into a raging enthusiasm by a deity." Some said Ann's excessive zeal for religion had now reached the feverish point of fanaticism. Fanatics often possess a mysterious fascination, and certainly that was true of Ann Lee. She could throw the repressed people who were attracted to her into orgies of enthusiasm or indignation. All their dammed-up feelings, their anger at the upper classes, their longing for a better life, were released by her magnetic powers.

Soon bizarre tales began to circulate around Manchester about the Shakers. They were accused of weird behavior, not just shouting and shaking but also frenzied dancing, speaking in tongues, and even witchcraft. The public was aroused, as it always is, by fear of the unknown. As the rumors escalated, charges of fanaticism and heresy led to public abuse of Ann Lee and her followers.

With the increase of danger, some of the new members "fell away" but those who remained grew stronger in their convictions and in their devotion to their flamboyant leader. A *Summary View* puts it this way:

> The powerful testimony Ann maintained against all sin, together with the wonderful operations of the Spirit of God which prevailed in the meetings of her little society, excited public attention, and stirred up the malignant feelings of many, of almost every class and description, to such a degree of enmity that, by formal opposition and tumultuous mobs, open persecution and secret malice, her very life seemed many times in great jeopardy.

Shaker history is filled with Ann Lee's cliff-hanging escapes from her tormentors. Once she was chased by an angry mob that knocked her down with clubs,

35

kicked and reviled her until "a certain nobleman," who was passing by on his horse, stopped and rescued her. Another time she escaped her pursuers by lying all night on the ice of a frozen pond. She was chilled to the bone but because of her "great peace and consolation" did not even take cold. In another crisis, a friendly neighbor saved her from harm by hiding her beneath a pile of wool in an attic.

Through all vicissitudes, Ann never wavered in her conviction that she was protected by Providence. When one of her own brothers, who felt disgraced by her public behavior, tried to punish her, she said God intervened. Here is her account of their remarkable confrontation.

So he [her brother] brought a staff, about the size of a large broom handle; and came to me while I was sitting in my chair, and singing by the power of God. He spoke to me; but I felt no liberty to answer. "Will you not answer me?" said he.

He then beat me over my face and nose, with his staff, till one end of it was much splintered. But I sensibly felt and saw the bright rays of the glory of God, pass between my face and his staff, which shielded off the blows, so that he had to stop and call for drink.

While he was refreshing himself, I cried to God for His healing power. He then turned the other end of his staff, and began to beat me again. While he continued striking, I felt my breath, like healing balsam, streaming from my mouth and nose, which healed me, so that I felt no harm from his stroke, but he was out of breath, like one which had been running a race.

No wonder Ann's followers began to say she had Godlike powers. They claimed she was the woman described in the Book of Revelations who was "clothed with the sun and crowned with the stars." That was going too far. "Blasphemy!" cried the authorities — and locked her up again.

This time they were taking no chances with Ann Lee. They put her in solitary confinement in a tiny cell of the stone prison and kept her locked up without food or water for two weeks. When they finally unlocked her door, after fourteen days of total deprivation, they expected to find her dead on the stone floor. But to their surprise, Ann Lee was alive and well. Those who watched her walk out were speechless. They thought they were witnessing a miracle; surely no one could survive such an ordeal without supernatural intervention.

There had been intervention all right, but it was not supernatural. What her persecutors did not understand was the devotion of Ann's followers. A dedicated youth named James Whittaker, who had been brought up by Ann Lee, somehow found access to her prison door. Each night, at great risk, he slipped into the jail and stealthily pushed the stem of a pipe through the keyhole of her cell; into the bowl he poured milk mixed with wine, and Ann had survived on the liquid she sipped from that pipe.

The Shakers thought the jailer's inability to keep Ann locked up was symbolic. One of their earliest hymns expresses the idea:

We're children of the free woman
We're free'd from the bondage of sin and death.
If we have any bands a-binding on us
We must break them and break them
And burn them up.

This song, like the other Shaker spirituals, was sung without accompaniment and with insistent, hypnotic rhythm that created the eerie atmosphere of another world.

5

The Female Christ

God is our infinite Mother. She
will hold us in her arms of blessedness
and beauty forever and ever.
—THEODORE PARKER, American Theologian (1810–1860)

MIRACLES ABOUND IN SHAKER HISTORY, SOME WITH
rational explanations, some without. But none is as
incredible as the concept, so central to Shaker
thought, that Ann Lee was the female Christ. This
is, surely, the most difficult part of Ann Lee's story
to grasp.

The astonishing idea of a female divinity seems
to have evolved from two sources. Ann's youthful
conditioning in the Wardley Movement, and her
mystical visitations. Jane and James Wardley had
instilled in Ann their belief that Jesus' second coming would be in the form of a woman, because they
were convinced that God had to be *both* male and
female. They said that the Christ spirit which had

first appeared in a man, Jesus, would eventually reappear, to fulfill the Biblical promise of the second coming, in the form of a woman. "Thereby," they prophesied, "God would shake the foundations."

It is essential to understand that at no time did the Shakers actually *worship* either Jesus or Ann Lee. Rather, both were held in deep reverence as the first elders of the Millennial Church, phenomenal beings to be loved and emulated.

The very suggestion that the Messiah might have a feminine aspect was incredible in a day when women were kept totally subservient. English women were obliged to marry, submit to their husband's commands, bear countless children, and remain always tethered to the home. The rights of women had not advanced one iota since the Tenth Commandment listed a man's wife as one of his possessions, along with his ox and his ass.

Jane and James Wardley rejected the prevailing prejudice against women. Over and over they said God had a dual nature. On one side was the eternal Father, symbolized by Jesus; on the other was the eternal Mother, symbolized by a holy woman yet to be chosen by Jesus.

After Ann's next arrest, she was not taken to jail but to a madhouse, a rat-infested place of horror whose inmates suffered from hideous cruelties. It was while she was there that she had an ecstatic experience that convinced her the Wardleys' prediction had finally come true. She was on her knees in her cell, praying to God for help when, suddenly, rays of light broke in upon her and "the glories of heaven" shone about her. A *Summary View* states as a fact: "She saw the Lord Jesus Christ in his glory." In that sublime moment, Ann claimed that Jesus revealed to her that *she* was his anointed successor on earth. He told her she must carry his Truth to the world and promised her divine protection. Henceforth, she was to be the incarnation of the word of God, the second coming of *Christ as a woman.*

In her mystical ecstasy, Ann was certain that the spirit of Christ suffused her being. Her identification with him was complete. "I feel the blood of Christ running through my soul and body!" she cried. "I feel him present with me, as sensibly as I feel my hands together . . . It is not I that speak. It is Christ who dwells in me."

As soon as Ann was released, she told her followers of her incredible visitation. She, Ann Lee of Toad Lane, had been miraculously changed into Ann, The Word of God Made Manifest in The World. *Testimonies* describes the riveting effect Ann's transfiguration had upon her associates.

When she was released from her imprisonment, and came to reveal to the society these last extraor-

dinary manifestations, so great was the display
of divine light with which her soul was filled and
so mighty the power of God which accompanied
her testimony, and so keen the searching power
of her spirit in discovering and bringing to light
the hidden works of darkness, that every soul was
struck with astonishment and filled with fear and
trembling. They saw at once that the candle of
the Lord was in her hand, and that she was able
by the light thereof, to search every heart, and try
every soul among them. From this time she was
received and acknowledged as the first visible
leader of the church of God upon earth.

The Wardleys were quick to confirm Ann's new
role. They announced that Ann Lee was indeed the
female Christ they had long awaited.

What are we to make of a woman who is known
to her followers as the female Christ? When a person completely identifies herself with her ideal, many
assessments are possible, from total dedication, to
wish fulfillment, to mental aberration, to hallucina-
tion, to insanity. As a rule, people who believe they
are touched by the divine are megalomaniacs gripped
by insane ideas of their own power. This was never
the case with Ann Lee. Throughout her life she
remained a modest woman who refused to exalt herself. She did not seek acclaim; her followers bestowed
it upon her. Mother Ann's mystical transformation

did not cause her to lose touch with the real world, nor did it alienate her from her true identity. On the contrary, after she had been hailed as "the Female Christ," Ann developed new strengths. Her personality grew more powerful, and her effectiveness in her world greatly increased.

Years later that devout nineteenth-century Shaker, Aurelia Mace, explained why it was possible for the Shakers to accept Ann Lee's extraordinary title of Female Christ: "To us God is Father *and* Mother and has been from the beginning. Jesus was an inspired man. Ann Lee was an inspired woman. Inasmuch as Jesus became the Christ, so may all be in possession of the same spirit."

In other words, spiritual perfection is a possibility open to all seekers after God's truth. Ann Lee was not Christ, nor did she claim to be. She was, instead, completely absorbed by His spirit and was therefore His female counterpart.

Many in Manchester were appalled by this startling new aspect of Ann's crusade. She had made enemies by asking people to desert family life and join a celibate sisterhood and brotherhood. That was bad enough. But when she described the closeness of her bond with her Savior by saying, "It is not I that speak; it is Christ who dwells in me," the good burghers of the town were shocked. The more they protested, the more extravagant her rhetoric became.

Testimonies says she announced: "I have been in fine vallies with Christ as a lover. I am married to the Lord Jesus Christ. He is my head and my husband, and I have no other! I have walked, hand and hand, with him in heaven." Ann's total acceptance of the in-dwelling presence of the Christ spirit was by now complete.

"Blasphemy!" cried the Manchester authorities. Again they meant it. This time when they arrested her they threatened to brand her on the cheek and bore her tongue with a hot poker. They dragged her before a tribunal of four ministers of the established church "with a view to obtain judgment against her." But the judges wanted to hear Ann and they asked her to speak for herself.

Speaking was Ann's forte. According to one legend, she spoke to them in twelve languages, including Greek, Latin, Hebrew, and French. In another version she spoke in seventy-two different tongues. Regardless of these fantastic tales, Shaker history states as a fact that "she spoke, and manifested such evident power of God, that they thought proper to dismiss her; and admonished her accusers to let her alone and not abuse her."

Testimonies describes in chilling terms what happened to Ann after that:

Enraged and disappointed at not being able to enlist these ministers against her, her persecutors

44

were determined to take the power of judgement
into their own hands, and became at once her
judges and executioners, and agreed to stone her
as a blasphemer. Accordingly they led her down
into a valley, without the town, where she was
followed by four of her brethren, namely, William
Lee, James Whittaker, Daniel Whittaker, and
James Shepard. Her persecutors having provided
themselves with a sufficient quantity of stones,
suitable for their purpose, they placed themselves
on the side of the hill, at a convenient distance,
and began to throw their stones; but not being
able, after repeated trials, to hit her or any of her
companions (except Daniel Whittaker, who received a slight wound on one of his temples), they
fell into contention among themselves, and finally
abandoned their design.

One might suppose that a woman in danger of
being stoned to death would be filled with rage and
fear. Not Ann Lee. "While they were throwing their
stones," she said, "I felt myself surrounded with the
presence of God, and my soul was filled with love.
I knew they could not kill me, because my work was
not done; therefore I felt joyful and comfortable,
while my enemies felt distress and confusion."

After this crisis, oddly enough, the persecution of
the Shakers in Manchester abated. Perhaps Ann and
her followers became more circumspect about con-
ducting their exuberant worship — "singing and danc-

ing, shaking, and shouting, speaking with new tongues and prophesying" — in public. Or perhaps Ann's enemies were intimidated because, as *Testimonies* states with simple faith: "They saw that she was evidently protected and supported, and her life preserved, by some interposing power." Whatever the reason, Ann Lee and her little band were, for a time, allowed to pursue their religion in peace.

Mother Ann, as she was now called, "always stood ready to obey the call of God." She did not relax when her life grew calmer. Quite the contrary. It was at this juncture that she embarked on the most ambitious project of her entire life.

News of the English colonies in America had filtered back to Toad Lane. It was rumored that freedom, especially freedom from coercion by church or state, was so vital to the Americans that they were ready to fight the British for it. Ann's active imagination was stimulated by what she heard. Fighting was anathema to the Shakers, but they yearned for freedom. How wonderful it would be to escape from a world where a person could be put to death for "unacceptable" religious opinions.

When the Reverend George Whitefield returned from his fifth trip to America, he again came to Manchester to preach. With blazing eloquence, Whitefield described the opportunities for a rebirth of the spirit in America. Ann Lee, who had never been out of Manchester, was deeply impressed by his descriptions of the new world. She began to think seriously about going there.

When Mother Ann meditated on a subject, mystical revelations often followed. She had a vision that the true church was to be established in America. She "saw" that the colonies would one day gain their independence and then freedom of conscience would be secured for all people to worship God without "hinderance or molestation." She said she saw a chosen people waiting for her in New England and she knew then that God wanted her to take the Millennial Church to America and that He would aid her in this enormous undertaking.

Other members of the Society had signs and visions that confirmed Ann's daring idea. One night, when a little group of Believers was resting by the roadside after a twenty-mile walk, a mysterious vision appeared to young James Whittaker. He saw a large tree "whose leaves," he said, "shone with such a brightness as made it appear like a burning torch." Whittaker took this to mean that he was to help Ann Lee plant the tree of faith in the new world. Mother Ann never forgot his image of the shining tree of faith and she later adopted it as a Shaker symbol.

A meeting was called to discuss the possibility of a trip to America. One after another, the Shakers rose to testify to the divine summons. Ann Lee said of that evening: "There were so many gifts in confirmation of our going — such as prophecies, revelations, visions and dreams — that some could hardly wait for others to tell their gifts and we had a joyful meeting and danced till morning."

And so the mission to the New World was set. Mother Ann would lead it, accompanied by those members of the society "who felt any special impressions on their own minds so to do." Despite their earlier enthusiasm, only eight Shakers had the determination and fortitude needed for this journey into the unknown, and three of them were members of Ann's family. They were Abraham Stanley, her husband; William Lee, her brother; Nancy Lee, her niece; and John Hocknell with his son Richard; James Whittaker, Mary Partington, and James Shepard. It is remarkable that Mother Ann's much abused husband elected to go with her. He must have decided a celibate marriage was preferable to a life without his vibrant wife.

Even the intrepid Mother Ann was apprehensive about the dangers that lay ahead. She said, "I know fresh scenes of trial and bitter persecutions await me in America, still my obedience to the call gives me power to comply." The others were fearful, too, but they placed their trust in Mother Ann. One proof of her power as a leader is the fact that after she left

England, the Shakers dwindled away to nothing. From then on Shakerism was to be purely an American phenomenon.

It seems almost unbelievable that a simple, uneducated woman could lead such a dangerous venture into unknown realms. Ann Lee might easily have given up and succumbed to the hopelessness that suffocated men and women in the Manchester slums. Instead, burdened by poverty and ignorance though she was, she somehow managed to pull together this small band of followers to seek a new life in a new world where, eventually, they would leave their mark. How, one must ask, could such a thing happen?

Leila Taylor and Anna White, in their book *Shakerism: Its Meaning and Message,* pose the question and give the Shakers' answer: "Why was Ann Lee so unlike the other poor women of Manchester, her neighbors in Toad Lane? Because she listened for the voice of God and obeyed his call."

6

The New World

Put your hands to work and your hearts to God.
—Mother Ann Lee

After the great decision to transport the Shaker faith to America, excitement ran high. It was a prodigious undertaking, but Mother Ann and her eight disciples were excited by the challenge. She commissioned John Hocknell to look for a ship whose passage they could afford. Hocknell was the right one to send. He was the only one of the group who had any money and he apparently financed the others. Without his help, the Shakers never could have left England.

Although most of the Believers were poor, they were lucky enough to find two well-to-do sponsors at critical moments in their early history. The first one was John Townley, a wealthy Manchester builder who had, at the very beginning of the movement, invited the Wardleys to live in his home on Canon Street and conduct their meetings under his protection. The second sponsor was Townley's brother-in-law, John Hocknell, who made the American voyage possible.

Hocknell, a man of property from Cheshire, was so enthusiastic about the Shaker ideal of communal living that he asked some of the impoverished members to move into his house, an invitation which infuriated his wife Hannah. She and her brothers, described as "high spirited people," had him arrested and put in jail. But after Hocknell was tried and released, Hannah, whose anger must have been fleeting, announced that she was going to join the Society of Believers herself. Although Sister Hannah Hocknell became a devout Shaker, she nonetheless refused to accompany her husband and their son Richard when they decided to make the hazardous journey to America.

Brother Hocknell managed to book inexpensive passage for the nine Shakers aboard the sailing ship *Mariah*. He felt compelled, however, to tell Ann Lee why it was cheaper than the other ships. The *Mariah* had been condemned. This bad news did not dismay the imperturbable Mother Ann. "God would not condemn it," she said, "while we are on it."

When Captain Smith, the skipper of the *Mariah*,

saw his unusual passengers he must have had some misgivings, but Ann Lee was quick to reassure him. A *Summary View* says: "Before they embarked, Mother Ann told the captain that he would not have whereof to accuse them, except it were concerning the law of their God." This turned out to be literally true.

It is almost impossible for a person accustomed to the speed and comfort of twentieth-century travel to imagine a voyage across the ocean in 1774. The tiny wooden ships were stinking and unventilated; the unrefrigerated food was nearly inedible; and the bathing and toilet facilities were almost nonexistent. Unreliable maps, unpredictable winds and weather, and a total lack of communication with the outside world made for a long and dangerous trip.

The *Mariah* sailed out of Liverpool on May 19, 1774, on a spring tide with the brave little band of Shakers on board. A feeling of relief must have swept over them as they looked for the last time on the land they were leaving. They were escaping from cruel and continuous persecution. Full of hope, they turned their thoughts toward the new world where, they had been told, religious freedom was the right of every human being.

It is easy to visualize Ann Lee standing resolutely at the ship's rail in her blue-and-white checked dress. We know that is what she wore on the trip because a swatch of the cotton material has been preserved and is now on display at the Shaker Museum in Chatham, New York, along with a flower-bordered teacup and saucer she is said to have brought with her, fragile eighteenth-century relics of a rugged pilgrimage.

The *Mariah* usually took three months to cross the Atlantic, or longer if the weather was bad. Mother Ann Lee knew how to make use of the time. As soon as the ship was riding the waves she began organizing religious services. Each day the Shakers spent hours worshipping in their unorthodox fashion. At first the sailors were entertained by the praying, preaching, singing, dancing, and shouting of their peculiar passengers. But when Mother Ann began to pour her preaching talents into testifying against the wickedness of the crew, they protested. Captain Smith ordered all services stopped at once. Mother Ann ignored him and continued to pray loudly for the men of the *Mariah*. The captain, used to obedience on board his ship, was enraged. He threatened to put all the Shakers in irons, and if that did not stop the preaching and praying, he vowed he would have them cast into the sea.

Mother Ann feared God far more than she feared Captain Smith. The next day she conducted worship as usual, with special prayers for all seafaring sinners. The captain, shouting with anger, again threatened to have them thrown overboard. But before any action could be taken, fate — and Mother Ann — intervened. A *Summary View* describes the emergency in dramatic terms.

It was in the evening, in the time of a storm; and the ship suddenly sprung a leak, occasioned by the starting of a plank between wind and water. The water now flowed in so rapidly, that notwithstanding all their exertions at the pumps, it gained upon them so fast that the whole ship's crew were greatly alarmed. The captain turned pale as a corpse, and said they must all perish before morning, for he saw no possible means to save the ship from sinking.

Mother Ann said, "Captain, be of good cheer. There shall not a hair of our heads perish. We shall all arrive safe to America. I just now saw two bright angels of God standing by the mast, through whom I received this promise."

She then encouraged the seamen, and she and her companions zealously assisted at the pumps. Shortly after this, a large wave struck the ship with great violence, and the loose plank was instantly closed to its place.

Whether this remarkable incident was effected by the violent force of the wave against the plank, or by some other unaccountable means, it was then viewed by all on board as a miraculous interposition of Divine Providence in their favor. The

Believers were soon in a great measure released
from the pumps; and the captain after this, gave
them free and full liberty to worship God according to the dictates of their own consciences, and
promised that he would never molest them again.
He was faithful to his promise, and treated them
with kindness and respect during the remainder of
the voyage, and declared afterwards that had it
not been for these people, he should have been
sunk in the sea, and never reached America.

Running through this story of supernatural rescue
at sea are the two golden threads woven into the
fabric of all Shaker history: faith in God and zest for
hard work. Ann Lee did not rely on the promise of
help from the two bright angels; she manned the
pumps as well. Linking hard work to devout worship
was a vital aspect of Shaker belief. "Put your hands
to work and your hearts to God" was the motto of
Mother Ann's life, and the firm foundation on which
she built the Shaker movement.

During their seventy-nine days at sea, the Shakers
had ample time to discuss how they would cope with
the problems ahead of them. The future was in every
way uncertain. They did not know where they would
live, how they would find work, or where they would
be able to establish their religious community; but
they had faith that God would unfold these things
for them. They could not even imagine one of the

biggest difficulties they were going to encounter: the Revolutionary War.

An early Shaker Hymn, "Voyage to Canaan," although clearly symbolic (sin is referred to as "that dreadful ocean") seems to recall the end of the Believers' epic voyage on the *Mariah*.

> *The passengers united*
> *In order peace and love;*
> *The wind all in our favour,*
> *How sweetly we do move!*
> *Let tempests now assail us,*
> *And raging billows roar,*
> *We will sweep thro' the deep,*
> *Till we reach the blessed shore.*

On August 6, 1774, the *Mariah* finally sailed into New York harbor. What a vast relief for all on board! After a perilous crossing on a crowded, leaking, and condemned ship, they must have been exhausted. One can imagine the mixture of thanksgiving, excitement, and anxiety that gripped the travelers when at last the eight church steeples of New York appeared on the horizon.

Undaunted as ever, Mother Ann led her little band ashore. They were poor English immigrants in a strange land where people were turning against the English. They had no friends in America and no immediate means of support. But they did have something they had not known in the squalor of Manchester. They had hope.

New York City was very different from that smoky factory town where Ann Lee was born. It was a pleasant place filled with trees and gardens. Most New Yorkers lived below Wall Street. North of Washington Square were farmhouses, grazing cattle, and country lanes. Down Fifth Avenue from Twenty-first Street flowed a sparkling brook where trout could be caught, while duck and quail shooting abounded along the banks of the Hudson.

But in many ways New York was becoming sophisticated. With a population of twenty thousand, it was the third largest city in the colonies, after Boston and Philadelphia. King's College (later Columbia University), the New York Hospital, and the Public Library had already been established. Under British leadership the city had acquired streetlights, a postal service, a newspaper, and a fire department, as well as prisons and poorhouses. One thing that was new to the Shakers — and horrifying — was the public slave market where black men, women, and children were sold from an auction block. To Mother Ann, who *knew* that every human being was a child of God, the slave trade was incomprehensible and utterly sinful.

On that quiet Sunday afternoon in August, the nine Believers walked up Broad Way and turned into

Queen Street (now Pearl Street) looking for lodgings. According to Shaker history, they stopped at a house occupied by a family named Cunningham. The mistress of the house was sitting outside to escape the heat. She must have been dumbfounded when Mother Ann stepped up to her, called her by name, and made the startling announcement, "I am commissioned by the Almighty God to preach the everlasting gospel to America, and an Angel commanded me to this house and to make a home for me and my people."

There is no record of Mrs. Cunningham's reply, but she was apparently moved by the conviction and the magnetism of her strange visitor, because the Cunningham family welcomed the travelers and Ann and her husband moved in with them. By happy coincidence, Mr. Cunningham was a blacksmith and Abraham Stanley was able to work in his smithy. *Testimonies* adds: "Mother Ann employed herself in washing and ironing for her living, and by her meekness, humility, and amiable deportment, she gained the love and esteem of the woman of the house by whom she was treated with great kindness." Ann Lee and Abraham Stanley remained with the Cunninghams over a year.

The other Shakers also found menial jobs and places to board. All believed their meager living arrangements were temporary, because Mother Ann promised them that if they endured their present poverty and suffering without turning from God, He would reward them in the future. If their trust in Mother's word ever wavered, they kept it quiet. Repeatedly she charged them to seek God's guidance. "God's world must be learned," she said, "much as a trade is learned. You have to work at it. God's grace can give us faith, but we must be as simple as a child to make that faith our own and live by it."

In America, as in England, Ann Lee's life was entirely God-centered. Everything else was secondary, including her husband. She continued to believe that the true source of human corruption was sex. No one could reach God, she declared, while wallowing in the lust of the flesh. Abraham Stanley, having endured her sexual abstinence for six years, began to spend his nights drinking. When he was drunk he shouted and cursed Ann for adopting a crazy religion that made her refuse to sleep with her husband.

Mother Ann tried to explain that her natural instincts had died away in love of God, but the more she talked of "the exuberant bliss of Divine intercourse," the more he drank. Ann, deeply absorbed in her pursuit of the Spirit, bore her husband's intoxicated abuse with patience but their "marriage" was becoming intolerable. In colorful detail A *Summary View* describes the turning point in their peculiar relationship.

Abraham Stanley was visited with a severe sickness. To nurse and take care of him required Mother Ann's whole time and attention. This duty she performed with the utmost care and kindness, tho often at the expense of great sufferings on her part. Their earnings now ceased, and they were reduced to extreme poverty.

Abraham at length recovered his health, so as to be able to walk the streets; and tho he never had been considered as a faithful and substantial Believer; yet he had hitherto supported his credit and reputation, and maintained an outward conformity to his faith. But on regaining his health, and before he was fully able to return to his occupation, he began to associate with the wicked at public houses, and soon lost all sense and feeling of religion, and began to oppose Mother Ann's testimony in a very ungodly manner, and urged her to renounce it, and live in sexual cohabitation, like the rest of the world. She replied, that she was willing to do any thing for him which justice, reason, or humanity required; but she should never consent to violate her duty to God; and endeavored to prevail on him to return to his duty and be faithful.

But as Abraham was determined to pursue the course of the world, he continued his vicious practice, instead of returning to his occupation, and left Ann to provide for herself. At length he brought a lewd woman into the house to her, and declared that, unless she would consent to live in sexual cohabitation with him, he would take that woman for his wife.

Ann replied with great firmness and resolution, that she would not do it if he should take her life as a consequence of her refusal. She also informed him in plain terms, that she considered his cruel and abusive conduct as a very unjust requital for the uniform kindness and attention which she had paid to him, both in sickness and in health; and she said she was still willing to take the most tender care of him, if he would return to his duty, and conduct himself as he ought to do, and urged him, in the most feeling manner, to return to the obedience of his faith; but all to no effect. He soon went off with the woman, to a distant part of the city, and it was reported that he was shortly after married to her.

Thus ended Ann Lee's thirteen years of marriage to Abraham Stanley. Exactly how the bonds of matrimony were dissolved we have no way of knowing. But we do know from then on she was thrown entirely upon her own resources, a critical situation for a woman in the eighteenth century.

During that winter Mother Ann endured "deep sorrow of the soul." Her children were dead. Her husband had departed. Her mission to America seemed doomed. Despite repeated statements of her faith in God's help, the chilling fact remained that she and her little group were stifled by poverty, privation, even hunger. In those bleak days she tasted the bitterness of despair. *Testimonies*, describing Mother Ann's plight, paints a doleful picture of her praying in a barren room with "a cold stone for a seat, and her only morsel a cruse of vinegar" and then adds: "Mother Ann sat down upon the stone, without any fire, sipped her vinegar and wept."

7

Escape to the Wilderness

And to the woman were given two
wings of a great eagle that she
might fly into the wilderness.
—*Revelations,* Chapter 12, verse 14

MOTHER ANN DID NOT STAY BOGGED DOWN IN DESPAIR;
her nature was too buoyant for that. One of her
colorful comments, preserved in the records of her
followers, was addressed to a man steeped in self-
pity. "Hold up your head," she told him. "God
made man upright. Don't lean against walls. You
walk crooked. Be cheerful! Be cheerful!"

With that same spirit Ann Lee pulled herself
together after her husband left her. She would not
think about her own troubles. She would concen-
trate on the immense, seemingly impossible, task
of establishing the Shaker faith in America.

It was the worst of times for such a venture. The
Believers had accomplished nothing in the year

they had spent in this country and now war was closing in on them. The summer of 1775 was turbulent in New York City. Patriots were inflamed by the Battle for Bunker Hill which had been fought that June in Boston. It was a victory for the British; but what a victory! King George III could not afford to subdue many more American "farmers" at such a cost.

Acts of violence against the hated British Tories were increasing throughout the Colonies. In New York, a troop of Americans rode to the shop of a Loyalist printer, smashed his presses, and carried off his type. Tories were persecuted, and in one instance a Tory woman was carried about on a rail by patriot women. A resolution passed by the Town Meeting in Boston told the story: "The whole United Colonies are upon the verge of a glorious revolution. We have seen petitions to the king rejected with disdain. For the prayer of peace, he has tendered the sword; for liberty, chains; for safety, death. Loyalty to him is now treason to our country."

Treason is a dire word. Clearly these were dangerous days for a tiny band of British pacifists struggling to bring forth God's kingdom in America. Mother Ann realized her only hope was to gather her scattered group and leave New York. As *A Summary View* says, "religious freedom was dearer to her than life." She was determined to achieve that freedom for her people at all costs.

Once again Mother Ann turned to John Hocknell for help. He agreed that a move was urgent. He had a little money left and had heard that land was cheap in the upstate town of Albany, so he boarded a sloop and sailed up the river to investigate.

Although everything outside Albany, except the tiny hamlet of Schenectady, was wilderness and Indians, Albany itself was a charming settlement built on three hills beside the beautiful Hudson River. Hocknell liked it at once and was sorely disappointed when he could find no land within his means. Then, according to Shaker legend, a most peculiar thing happened. He was praying for guidance when, suddenly, his arm rose of its own accord and his finger pointed toward the northwest. Following this strange lead, he went in that direction to see what he could find.

Whether or not this odd event actually occurred, the fact is Hocknell did discover a promising tract of woods eight miles northwest of Albany. Since it was remote property belonging to a wealthy patroon named Stephen Van Rennsselaer, he hoped he could purchase it with ease. John Hocknell, devout Shaker, must have been awed when he called on the Lord of the Manor Rensselaerwyck in his elegant brick home beneath the drooping elms. Van Rensselaer, like the other patroons, had received his huge estate from the Dutch when they owned New York; and his manor house, built as a gift for his bride, was considered one of the handsomest residences in the colonies.

Squire Van Rensselaer listened to Hocknell with interest. No, he would not sell that wilderness property — christened Niskeyuna by the Indians — but he agreed to lease it to the Shakers "in perpetuity." Many references say Niskeyuna means "Good Corn Land," which is incorrect. It means "Where The Water Flows," and in the eighteenth century the property included a winding river, now reduced to a choked stream. This area was called Watervliet by the Dutch and later given the "spiritual name" Wisdom Valley by the Shakers.

A jubilant Hocknell returned to New York to tell Mother Ann about the land he had leased for the Shakers. She was elated, especially when he described the isolation of Niskeyuna. At long last the Believers were going to find security in seclusion. Now God would make their dream come true. Withdrawing from the world into a community of their own, they would be able to establish the Millennial Church. It was an incredibly ambitious undertaking.

Mother Ann wanted to move to Niskeyuna at once, but John Hocknell said that was impossible. First he must return to England to get his wife and the rest of his family and, he added, "make further arrangements for the settlement of the Society in this country." In plain words, that meant raising more money. Ann's brother, William Lee, who was working as a blacksmith, and James Whittaker, now employed as a weaver, would contribute all the cash they could raise for the move to Niskeyuna, but much more was needed.

One can only marvel at John Hocknell's energy and dedication. He made the long journey back to England, sold all his property, packed up his ex-Methodist family, and brought them to America to join a struggling religious group in a journey to the wilderness. At that time John Hocknell was seventy years old.

While Hocknell was away, William Lee and James Whittaker spent all the time they could spare on the back-breaking task of clearing the newly acquired land. An impatient Mother Ann made several journeys up the river that autumn to inspect Niskeyuna and urge them to make haste. The sooner the Shakers could leave New York City, the better. They could already feel the hot breath of Revolution on their necks.

Christmas day, 1775, John Hocknell and his family landed in Philadelphia, bringing with them the John Partington family to join the Shaker adventure. They proceeded to New York City by land and went at once to Mother Ann, who welcomed them with open arms. Now she and her disciples could finally begin the big move to Niskeyuna. All had remained faithful to Mother except her rebellious husband, Abraham Stanley, who was heard of no more.

To go from New York to Albany in those days you consulted not a timetable but a calendar. In mild weather you went by boat, but when the Hudson was frozen, you went by stagecoach. Either way, it was a three-day trip. Because the Shakers had to transport all their supplies, they decided on the boat. Soon after the ice left the river they boarded a sloop bound for Albany.

They got out of New York just in time. Had they lingered, they would have been embroiled in the war. In the summer of 1776 American patriots were on the rampage. When a copy of the Declaration of Independence arrived from Philadelphia, General Washington had it read aloud at evening parade and the people went wild. In the hysteria that followed, a mob threw a rope around the statue of King George III and tugged it down. (The lead from his statue was later converted into anti-British bullets by the women of Litchfield, Connecticut.) In those violent days, nothing British was safe.

That August twenty-five thousand English soldiers led by General Howe landed in New York, backed by a powerful fleet under his brother, Lord Howe. The Howes forced George Washington, who had only eight thousand men, to abandon the city. Not long afterward, English frigates sailed into the Hudson. For the next seven years, New York City belonged to the British.

By conquering and holding the entrance to the Hudson River, the British hoped to cut the United Colonies in two and thus subdue them. To the Tories, the British army and navy were the king's answer to the traitorous Declaration of Independence. To the Shakers, both the American and British fighters were sinners desecrating God's law of "love thy neighbor as thyself."

The Believers were happy to be leaving the turmoil of the city behind them. Once more filled with hope, they stood on deck as their sloop sailed past the Palisade cliffs, the wild and wooded shores of Westchester, and the awesome Storm King Mountain. Their childlike trust in God gave them the kind of optimism that was expressed in the first Shaker hymn, "The Happy Journey."

The heavens of glory is our destination
We're swiftly advancing to that happy shore;
We're travelling on in regeneration,
And when we get through we shall sorrow no more.

This beautiful journey which we've undertaken,
Excels all the travel that ever has been,
And those that perform it will never be shaken,
Because it leads out of the nature of sin.

8

"Good Woman"

Do all your work as though you had
a thousand years to live; and as
you would if you knew you must die
tomorrow.

—MOTHER ANN LEE

WHEN MOTHER ANN OPENED THE FIRST SHAKER
colony at Niskeyuna in 1776 she was forty years old.
A short woman with proud bearing and penetrating
blue eyes, her hard life had made her strong. She was
able to work long hours with the men, clearing and
draining the land, building cabins with crude tools,
and planting crops under the burning sun. Like all
true leaders, Mother Ann never asked her people to
do anything she would not do herself.

The first months were frightening. Food was
scarce; insects and snakes from the nearby swamp
plagued the settlers; sickness and fever were rampant.
Mother Ann nursed the ill and heartened the discouraged. Nothing could dim her enthusiasm be-

cause at last she had found a sanctuary for her people. A *Summary View* describes the situation: "The place being then in a wilderness state, they began, with indefatigable zeal and industry, and through additional sufferings, to prepare the way for a permanent settlement, where they could enjoy their faith in peace, amid the tumults of the war in which the country was then involved."

The Shakers were in no way retreating from reality when they settled at Niskeyuna. Their innumerable hardships, as they struggled to establish a Utopian community on the edge of civilization, would have defeated them if they had been dreamers and not doers. Their very survival was in question. Of the many dangers they faced — scarcity of food, exposure to bad weather, illness, and wild animals — the most threatening may have been the Indians.

The immigrants from England had never seen Indians at close range. Naturally, they were afraid of their nearest neighbors the Mahicans. Known also as River Indians, the Mahicans were part of the Algonkian race. Since they had once owned Albany, they resented all white intruders. Mother Ann heard that the Mahicans (the name means "wolf") had beaten the Mohawks, murdering and scalping them, and then, after applying to the governor for free rum "to comfort our hearts," had demolished the French. It took considerable courage for her to approach them. But having dedicated her life to living in love and charity with her neighbors, she was not going to be put off by the mere fact that her neighbors happened to be fierce. Just as any housewife would do in England, Mother Ann put on her bonnet and went to call on the people next door.

The Mahicans must have been surprised when the energetic little woman with the blue eyes and warm smile arrived at their camp. Mother Ann was the kind of person who made an impression. A *Summary View* says, "Her manners were plain, simple, and easy, and she possesed a certain dignity of appearance that inspired confidence and commanded respect."

If only we knew more details of her confrontation with the Mahicans! It must have been a colorful scene. Shaker legend claims that through her "gift of tongues" she was able to converse with the Indians in their own dialect. However the meeting began, it ended with Mother Ann's sitting on the ground, smoking the peace pipe with her neighbors.

According to the Shakers, the Indians were the first to realize there was something strange about the leader of the little colony in the woods. One of the braves announced that he saw a "bright light" surrounding Mother Ann. "The Great Spirit has sent this woman to do much good," he said. From then on the Mahicans honored Mother Ann with the title of "Good Woman."

The "Good Woman's" friendship with her neighbors turned out to be crucial. The Shakers never could have survived their first year in the wilderness without the Indians' help. The Mahicans brought them gifts of food and taught them many things, from growing corn to tapping maples for syrup. They showed them how to weave baskets, make herbal medicines and dyes, and dry seeds, skills the Shakers were later to develop into fine arts. And when the white "Wolf Moon," as the Indians called the full moon of January, shone over the frozen countryside, it was the Mahicans who taught them how to trap wild animals for food, to fish through ice, and to protect themselves in below-zero weather.

No matter what hardships Mother Ann and her followers faced, memories of their escape from "the dark Satanic mills of Manchester" (as the poet William Blake described them) made their new life seem promising. To Mother Ann the wilderness was congenial. She had already journeyed, during those soul-searching years in England, to a much more frightening space — the wilderness within herself. Miraculously, she had discovered there the Christ spirit. She told her people over and over that they, too, must descend into their own interior spaces and find the gentleness of Christ which lay within each one of them. Only by making that inward journey could they prepare for the hardships that life was sure to bring them.

Mother Ann never doubted that the little Shaker settlement at Niskeyuna would eventually flourish, but some of the others were not so sure. To sustain their sagging morale, and to get the utmost out of every day, she required all Believers to follow a strict schedule. She knew instinctively that rigorous discipline can be extremely supportive to people living in a strange environment. It can give life a reliable framework and free the mind for other things. Mother Ann's daily regime left no time for self-pity or self-indulgence. The Shakers rose at daylight and worked continuously until dark, stopping at regular intervals to worship God and rejoice in the opportunity He had given them.

Mother Ann's evening prayer sessions, attended by weary men and women after a long day's labor, were never thought of as a "duty," but were anticipated with pleasure and enjoyed as refreshment. This is an important difference between the Shakers and their Puritan contemporaries. Both sects practiced the virtues of simplicity, austerity, hard work, and denial of the flesh, not for their personal gain but for the glory of God. Both believed self-denial had meaning only as it contributed to the salvation of the soul. But the Shakers relished life, while the Puritans permitted themselves as little pleasure as possible.

Since Shakers and Puritans alike thought the

world might end at any moment, they lived in constant awareness of their souls. The purpose of life was to prepare to meet one's Maker face to face. As Mother Ann said in one of her most quoted remarks, "Do all your work as though you had a thousand years to live, and as you would if you knew you must die tomorrow."

While the Puritans valued thought and denied feeling, the Shakers exalted feeling, so long as it was not sexual in nature. This is a paradox, since Puritans married and had children while Shakers, sworn to celibacy, rejected sex as the primary cause of sinfulness. The difference seems to lie in the word *joy*. For Puritans, joy was the handmaiden of sin; for Shakers, joy was the elixir of life. Puritans were forbidden to dance and sing. Shakers relished both. Their songs and dances, highly charged with emotion, were essential, not only as a way to worship God, but also for recreation and release from tension. Mother Ann must be given credit for Shakerism's early emphasis on jubilation. She insisted that dancing and singing were mysterious gifts from God that promoted unity among people of all kinds.

In the beginning, Shaker dancing and singing were formless. The impulsive whirlings and discordant shoutings later gave way to rhythmic chants, "step songs," "square order shuffles," and hymns of praise and thanksgiving. In dancing, as in everything else,

Shakers never mingled the sexes. Males and females faced each other in straight lines, advancing and retreating, marching and circling, but never, never touching. One of the earliest of the "Millennial Praises" expresses their simple joy in being together:

We love to dance, we love to sing,
We love to taste the living spring,
We love to feel our union flow,
While round, and round, and round we go.

God was at all times a powerful presence at Niskeyuna. Mother Ann made sure of that, as is clear in a graphic account of the Shakers' first Christmas in their new community, told in a booklet called *The Shaker Order of Christmas*, by Edward and Faith Andrews. Since the Believers did not deify Jesus, they were unsure how they should observe Christmas— until Mother Ann "received a sign" through John Hocknell's wife Hannah. It is a typical Shaker legend.

It was still dark when Hannah Hocknell awoke on that December morning in 1776. A cold wind was sweeping over the desolate swamp of bogs, wild grass, and weeds beside which the cabin stood, and rattling the branches in the surrounding forest. The deep slough-holes formed by the meandering Scherluyn Creek were already frozen,

and on this morning Hannah could hear occa-
sional flurries of sleet pelting against the cabin.

Rising from the husk mattress which served as
a bed, the elderly Shakeress lit a candle, started a
fire, and began to dress in preparation for her usual
day's work. To the world outside the Shaker settlement, it was Christmas morning. But to Hannah, as one who still followed the old-style Julian
calendar, it was in no wise different from other
mornings. She had sweeping to do, and washing for
the family of four sisters and six brethren. After
a simple breakfast of bean porridge and root tea
she would attend to these tasks, faithful to the in-
junction of Mother Ann Lee, the foundress of the
order, to put her hands to work and her heart to
God.

For some unaccountable reason, however, the
"old Believer" could not lace her shoes: a peculiar
shaking or agitation of the limbs hindered all her
efforts. She was still standing by the stove, bent
over, struggling for control, when Mother Ann herself, lamp in hand, appeared at the doorway.
Watching for a while, the prophetess was finally
moved to speak—from the Scriptures, as was so
often her wont:

"Try no longer, Hannah! Put off thy shoes from
off thy feet, for the place whereon thou standest
is holy ground."

Mother Ann recognized in Hannah's experience a "gift": that this was a holy day on which no

manual labor should be done, a day to be dedicated exclusively to cleaning the house of the spirit.

So originated the Shaker order of Christmas. Sister Hannah's resolution to do the washing and cleaning, and Mother Ann's inspiration as she stood at the door, led to the annual rituals of "The Open Door" and "The Opening of the Mind." From then on Shakers spent the days before Christmas in ceremonial sweeping and scrubbing to commemorate that first Christmas at Niskeyuna. As they scoured, they chanted work songs such as:

> *Sweep, sweep and cleanse your floor,*
> *Mother's standing at the door,*
> *She'll give us good and precious wheat,*
> *With which there is no chaff nor cheat.*

The cleansing, with real mops and with spiritual brooms, was to wash away all "stains of sin" in preparation for the great Shaker dream — the birth of the Christ spirit within every human heart.

The Believers at Niskeyuna were enlarging their forms of worship but not their numbers. It is said that only one thing is required to make a group expand: a strong leader. In Mother Ann the Shakers had that essential requisite, but still new members did not join their community. Because the Shakers placed primary importance on the conversion of others to their faith, this lack of new members was disheartening. In a world smothered by sin and darkness, they hoped to create a perfect order that would entice the "lost" to join them. How else could they act as pathfinders to God? Yet no new people came out to the little colony. As always, Mother Ann's faith was steadfast. *Testimonies* records her words to her followers in these times of deep despair:

> "O my dear children, hold fast and be not discouraged. God has not sent us to this land in vain, but He has sent us to bring the gospel to this nation which is deeply lost in sin; and there are great numbers who will embrace it, and the time draws nigh."

Elder William Lee then asked Mother, "Do you believe the gospel will ever open to the world?"

Mother replied, "Yea, Brother William, I certainly know it will, and the time is near at hand when they will come like doves."

William replied, "Mother, you have often told us so, but it does not come yet."

Mother said, "Be patient, be patient, O my dear children, for I can see great numbers coming now, and you will soon see them coming in great numbers."

And while they were thus downcast, Mother came out and led them into the forest west of their dwelling where, by the ministrations of the power and gifts of God, through Mother, they had a very joyful meeting, and praised God in songs and dances.

From day to day new converts were expected. When they did not appear the undiscouragable Mother Ann commanded her little family to build up their store of provisions. They obeyed her, but still nothing happened. "What is to be done with all this," they asked her, "seeing we are so retired from the world and have so small a company to consume it?"

Mother Ann replied firmly, "We shall have a great company before the close of another year. I see large numbers coming and they will accept and obey the gospel. I see great men come and bow down their heads and confess their sins. The time draws nigh!"

Another winter gripped the Shakers, more severe than any they had known. Biting cold and deep snow compounded their miseries; their living conditions were woefully inadequate for zero weather. At last, even Mother Ann sounded dejected. She stood by the icy stream and cried, "O that the fishes of the sea, and the fowls of the air and all things that live and breathe, yea, all the trees of the forest and grass of the fields would pray to God for me."

And *Testimonies* adds poignantly, "Her words were acompanied with tears and heartfelt agony, shared by all who were present."

9

We Do Not Lose Heart

> Therefore, having this ministry by
> the mercy of God, we do not lose
> heart.
>
> —11 *Corinthians* 4:1

IF TRUE HAPPINESS LIES IN DEVOTING ALL OF ONE'S powers to a cause one is completely committed to, Mother Ann at work in the wilds of Niskeyuna must have been deeply, satisfyingly happy. Winter and summer she labored without ceasing, exhorting the others to do the same. She wanted everything to be in readiness when the people "came like doves."

Mother Ann's idea of work-as-worship was both a doctrine and a daily discipline. "Be diligent with your hands," she said, "because Godliness does not lead to idleness." But she cautioned her followers never to overwork because that would exalt labor, not God. Only by keeping life simple, she told them, and cutting away all desire for personal gain, could they reach God.

81

The Believers eagerly followed Mother's example. They cultivated the land and they cultivated the spirit — but still no converts came to Niskeyuna. By the autumn of 1779 some of them were discouraged, others really depressed. Three years had passed since they sailed up the Hudson and opened their mission to the new world. No progress had been made and the future looked desolate.

Then, one March day in 1780, something did happen.

A great religious revival, lead by impassioned Baptists, was convened in New Lebanon, New York, a small town at the foot of the Taconic Mountains. Although the revival took place thirty miles southeast of Niskeyuna, it was to have a strong connection with the Shaker movement. All sorts of hopeful men and women — rough pioneers and college graduates, poor and well-to-do, old and young — traveled to New Lebanon seeking spiritual rejuvenation from the Baptists. Discouraged by the grimness of frontier life, frightened by the wreckage and havoc of war, guilt-ridden by feelings of sin, all were looking for the same thing: escape from a hard life. They wanted absolution for their sins and assurance of a better life in the next world.

Instead of salvation, they discovered that the New Lebanon revival was just another battlefield. An angry conflict raged between the "Old Lights" of the church, who believed people could be saved by faith alone, and the "New Lights" who believed salvation depended on good works. The struggle between the two groups was constant; only during worship did the debates cease.

The revival services were held in a barn belonging to a prosperous farmer named George Darrow. Day and night there was wild, exalted preaching and prophesying, accompanied by praying, singing, and shouting. Men and women, transported into religious ecstasies, would fall to the ground "as if wounded in battle." The worshippers were convinced the Millennium was near, the triumphant second coming of Christ that would heal their conflicts and solve their problems, uniting all factions in Christ.

But no Millennium arrived and the religious fever cooled. Many disillusioned revivalists left. Two who went west, Reuben Wight and Talmadge Bishop, became important in the Shaker story. When they reached Albany, Wight and Bishop heard strange tales about a group of "Believers" living in the woods with a female leader who was scornfully referred to as the "Elect Lady." With excited curiosity, the two men made a detour to Niskeyuna to investigate.

Mother Ann was waiting to give Reuben Wight and Talmadge Bishop a warm welcome. She said that because of a premonition she had been expecting them. She invited them to spend the night and join the Shakers in worship, which they did. The two visitors were amazed by everything they saw and heard. Is it possible, they asked, that the Christ we have waited for in vain actually *has* come, as these devout people claim — and in the form of a woman?

The Shakers' answer was a resounding *yes*.

"It is true," said Mother Ann. "I am the embodiment of the Christ spirit. But you, too, can experience that indwelling presence, if you will forsake the world and the flesh and let yourself be embued by His spirit and consumed by His love."

She told them there would never be a universal day of judgment for all mankind. Salvation is not an event, said Mother Ann. It is a quiet transformation that takes place within an individual who has entered wholly into the life of the spirit. For that person, the "world" and all its desires have come to an end, and the Millennium has begun.

When the visitors protested that such ideas amounted to revolution, Mother Ann replied, "We are the people who turn the world upside down."

Fired by her spiritual fervor, Wight and Bishop hurried back to New Lebanon to tell others about this extraordinary female. They described her as having the physical courage and spiritual strength of a male because the only way they could relate to such a powerful woman was to compare her to a man. In truth, Mother Ann was far more feminine than

she was masculine. A *Summary View* states enthusi-
astically: "By many of the world who saw her
without prejudice she was called beautiful; and to
her faithful children she appeared to possess a degree
of dignified beauty and heavenly love which they
had never before discovered among mortals."

Two leaders of the New Lebanon revival, the Reverend Joseph Meacham and the Reverend Samuel
Johnson, listened carefully to the glowing descriptions of the Shakers and their female "lead." They
decided to send one of their strongest associates,
Calvin Harlow, to Niskeyuna to interrogate Mother
Ann. They instructed Harlow carefully as to the
exact question he was to put to this strange woman
in the woods who claimed to be invested with the
authority of Christ.

The encounter between Calvin Harlow and
Mother Ann was an important one, and their words
have been preserved in Shaker history.

Calvin Harlow: "Saint Paul says, 'Let your women
keep silence in the Churches; for it is not permitted
unto them to speak, but they are commanded to
be under obedience, as also saith the law. And if
they will learn any thing, let them ask their husbands
at home; for it is a shame for a woman to speak in
the Church.' But you — you not only speak, you seem
to be an Elder in your Church. How do you recon-
cile this with the Apostle's doctrine?"

Mother Ann: "The order of nature requires a man and a woman to produce offspring . . . He is the Father and she is the Mother; and all the children, both male and female, must be subject to their parents . . . but when the man is gone, the right of government belongs to the woman. So it is with the family of Christ."

Calvin Harlow was apparently completely won over to the Shakers by his encounter with Mother Ann. Whether it was her bewitching personality or her reasoning that did it, we do not know. But he hurried back to New Lebanon and reported to the Reverend Mr. Meacham that the long-awaited Second Coming had indeed occurred. Joseph Meacham was dubious. He set out for Niskeyuna to see for himself this electrifying "woman of the new birth" and he took two other Baptists with him.

Meacham was a solid citizen, not given to fantasy. A forty-year-old Baptist minister from Enfield, Connecticut, he was a well-known religious leader. His confrontation with Mother Ann must have been a study in contrasts. When they met in the woods that morning in May, the stern American Baptist and his two brethren stood on one side and Mother Ann, small and dynamic, stood opposite them with her chief disciple, James Whittaker, at her side.

According to *Testimonies*, Brother Meacham said, "If you have attained to that of God which we have

The American Shakers

A Celibate, Religious Community

Coeval with the American Republic; First Shaker Family formed at Watervliet, N. Y., 1776 ; First organized Shaker Community established at New Lebanon, N. Y., 1788; Fifteen Shaker Societies in seven States of the United States of America.

Beginnings.

Founder, ANN LEE, of Manchester, England, (1736-1784). In religious revival of 17th Century, arose the "Shaking Quakers," or "Shakers," 1754. Nine persons from Manchester and Bolton, emigrated, May 1774, for the purpose of founding a Shaker Church in America. Eight remained faithful. They were ANN LEE, William Lee, James Whittaker, John Hocknell, James Shepherd, James Partington, Mary Partington, Nancy Lee.

FROM ANN LEE'S TEACHINGS.

Basic Principles of the Shaker Order,

VIRGIN PURITY, PEACE, JUSTICE, LOVE,

expressed in CELIBATE LIFE, NON RESISTANCE, COMMUNITY OF GOODS, UNIVERSAL BROTHERHOOD-- held to be the Divine Order of Society.

Resultant Beliefs and Practices Held as Ideals

TO BE ATTAINED IN THE INDIVIDUAL AND SOCIETY.

Equality of the Sexes, in all departments of life,
Equality in Labor, all working for each, and each for all,
Equality in Property,--No rich, no poor, Industrial Freedom,
Consecrated Labor, Dedicated Wealth, A United Inheritance,
Each using according to need,
Each enjoying according to capacity.
Freedom of Speech, Toleration in Thought and Religion. Often persecuted,
Shakers have never been known to persecute.
Abolition of all Slavery,--Chattel, Wage, Habit, Passion, Poverty, Disease.
Temperance in all things.
Justice and Kindness to all living beings.
Practical Benevolence. Thou shalt love thy neighbor as thyself.
True Democracy, Real Fraternity, Practical Living of the Golden Rule.

Religious Ideals and Worship.

All life and activity animated by Christian Love is Worship. Shakers adore God as the Almighty Creator, Fountain of all Good, Life, Light, Truth and Love,--the One Eternal Father-Mother.
They recognize the Christ Spirit, the expression of Deity, manifested in fulness in Jesus of Nazareth, also in feminine manifestation through the personality of Ann Lee. Both, they regard as Divine Saviors, anointed Leaders in the New Creation. All in whom the Christ consciousness awakens are Sons and Daughters of God. Spiritual man has, as his divine prerogative and highest destiny, to live in clear conception of and in active harmony with the Highest Good. The Life of the Spirit not the form of expression is essential.

Practical Issues.

Beautiful, comfortable Community Homes, in each a Christ Family.
Daily manual labor for all, according to strength and ability. "Hands to work and hearts to God." (*Ann Lee*)
Opportunity for intellectual and artistic development, within the necessary limits prescribed by the common good.
Sanitation, Health, Longevity
Simplicity in dress, speech and manner.
Purity in thought, speech and personal habits.
Freedom from debt, worry and competition.

Government.

No Government without God, No Body without a Head.
The Head of the Shaker Order is Christ. The Visible Human Representative is vested in a

DUAL ORDER OF LEADERS.

Spiritual Leaders, of both sexes, a Ministry over Societies, Elders over Families.
Temporal Leaders, of both sexes, Trustees, Deacons and Care-takers, in charge of Business and Industrial Interests.

The Inner Life,

according to the Shaker Faith, is twofold, embracing
Repentance--confessing and forsaking all sin;
Regeneration--the growth and unfoldment in the individual of the Christ Spirit, through living according to the teachings and practice of Jesus Christ. As opposed to the common life of human generation and selfish gratification, this is held to be the Resurrection Life.
Physical development, mental growth and spiritual unfoldment form the only rational basis for a harmonious and happy existence; self-denial the corner-stone of the structure. The truths inherent in Shakerism are the underlying truths of God life in all ages and the mission of the Shaker is to unfold and demonstrate these truths.

A broadside describing the Shaker history and belief.

not, we should be glad to share with you; for we want to find the best way to be saved."

Mother Ann designated Whittaker as her spokesman. "If you are to be saved by Christ," he said, "you must walk as he walked. And if you have committed sins, you must confess them to witnesses in whom Christ has taken up His abode."

"Are *you* perfect?" challenged Meacham. "Do you live without sin?"

Whittaker's answer was firm. "The Power of God does enable souls to cease from sin; and we have received that power. We have actually left off committing sin, and we live in daily obedience to the will of God."

Mother Ann could no longer keep silent. "Sin is gratification of self," she said. "Only through celibacy can true Godliness be achieved. You must forsake the marriage of the flesh, or you cannot be married to the Lamb."

The discussion continued all day, interrupted only for worship. By evening, the Reverend Mr. Meacham and his companions had also fallen under Mother Ann's spell. She offered them a program more exciting and more specific than anything they had found at the revival or within their own faith. Mother told them the Shaker requirements were precise. They must separate themselves from the material world, shun all sex, and confess all sins. Then, perhaps, by living in monastic simplicity and unity, they would be able to reach God in work and in worship. The cost was high — total denial of self; but the promised reward was great — at-oneness with God.

The Reverend Joseph Meacham, chief Baptist preacher in the district of New Lebanon, became Mother Ann's first important convert in America. She called him her "first-born son" and predicted that when she died Joseph Meacham would hold the Believers together. Meacham's wife and children, his father and other relatives also joined the Believers. The addition of children to the colony was vital since the society's prohibition against sex meant, of course, there would be no Shaker children to carry the United Society of Believers to the next generation.

The story of the Reverend Mr. Meacham's conversion spread rapidly and drew other seekers to Niskeyuna. Inspired by Mother Ann's eloquence, many of them became Shakers. Some were simple folk like Talmadge Bishop, others important people like George Darrow and the Reverend Samuel Johnson. Johnson, who graduated from Yale in 1769, was followed into the Shaker faith by his wife, Elizabeth. The reasons they gave for joining were interesting. Samuel Johnson said, "While at Niskeyuna I witnessed divine power. Listening to Mother Ann, my own conscience was salved and I received a true baptism of the Holy Spirit."

89

His wife's explanation seems to be more honest. Elizabeth Johnson said she had married a minister of the Gospel when she was twenty-four hoping "I would be living nearer to God, for the spirit of worship is strong within me." Instead she found disappointment in a marriage which seemed to keep her from God, and that was why she became "greatly interested in the self-denying way of these people called Shakers."

Other married couples also joined the Shakers, some bringing with them their children to be loved and cared for by the community. Why would husbands and wives want to belong to a sect that forbade sexual intercourse? Did they agree with Mother Ann that "the root of all human depravity is the sexual relationship originating with Adam and Eve?" Were they trying to avoid parenthood? Were some women seeking the equality with men which the Shakers, unlike the society around them, insisted upon? The questions are endless, the answers unclear.

But for the United Society of Believers nothing was unclear. They stated as a fundamental principle: "The object of Shaker life is self-conquest . . . It is to die to the corrupt, passionate animal life of the world that we may be resurrected in pure and angelic societies."

10

The Living Way: Celibacy and Separation of the Sexes

Near Albany they settled,
And waited for a while,
Until a mighty shaking
Made all the desert smile.
At length a gentle whisper,
The tidings did convey,
And many flocked to Mother,
To learn the living way.

—Early Shaker Spiritual

THE SHAKER COMMUNITY BEGAN TO EXPAND AFTER the New Lebanon revival. Mother Ann, watching over her flourishing colony, recalled the prophecy of Isaiah: "The wilderness and the solitary place shall be glad for them; and the desert shall rejoice and blossom as the rose." People were attracted to Niskeyuna by rumors that circulated about Mother Ann. It was said her faith was so intense that those who got near her could absorb it. Her easy conquest of the two prominent Yankee ministers, the Reverend Joseph Meacham and the Reverend Samuel Johnson, spread her fame for miles around, but it also aroused antagonism against her.

Many considered this strange woman a threat to society. Everything she stood for was dangerous: the rejection of creeds, liturgies, sacraments, and priesthood; the refusal to take oaths or bear arms; the promotion of communal living and common ownership of property; the insistence on the obvious (to her) fact that the gifts of preaching, teaching, and prophecy were available to women as well as to men. Scandalous suggestions, all of them, particularly in eighteenth-century America. But the most threatening of all was her open animosity toward marriage.

When Mother Ann announced that marriage was a stumbling block in the path to spiritual fulfillment she seemed to be undermining society itself. It made no difference that she said her convictions came from the Bible and quoted Saint Paul (1 Corinthians 7: 32-33): "He that is unmarried careth for the things that belong to the Lord, how he may please the Lord: But he that is married careth for things that are of the world, how he may please his wife."

Her ideas seemed nothing short of madness, even witchcraft to frontier folk on a rude frontier. People were enraged. They said any woman who was against the institution of marriage must be some kind of a devil. To which Mother Ann replied enigmatically, "The devil is a real being, as real as a bear. I know, for I have seen him and fought with him."

The Believers agreed with Mother Ann that

"weakness of the flesh" caused all sinfulness — vulgarity, coarseness, slothfulness, vanity, extravagance, greed, disorder, dishonesty. They thought her critics were the problem, not she, and they defended their leader fiercely. As Aurelia Mace explained in *The Aletheia*: "Mother called people away from selfish family life into a great brotherhood and sisterhood, and struck a deadly blow against those indulgences which the carnally minded so much desired."

Mother Ann herself did nothing to combat the hostility of her neighbors. *Testimonies* recounts one occasion when she "came into a room where there were a number of married men and their wives and said, 'I see a vision, a large black cloud rising as black as a thunder cloud, and it is occasioned by men sleeping with their wives.' Mother admonished them not to do it any more."

Another time she asked a woman with five children, "Are you not ashamed to live in the filthy works of the flesh? You must go and take up your cross and put your hands to work and your heart to God." (*Take up your cross* was a phrase the Shakers often used to refer to their renunciation of sex.) Such statements helped to ignite the already overheated atmosphere that surrounded her.

Of course Mother Ann knew the Shaker way was not for everyone. Of those who found celibacy impossible she said, again quoting Saint Paul, "If they cannot contain, let them marry: for it is better to marry than to burn." Often she showed an uncanny ability to put herself in another's place. According to *Testimonies*, a convert who had been married to the handsome, strong-minded Shakeress Lucy Wright, told Mother Ann it was out of the question for him to try to suppress his sexual desires. She answered him with great kindness: "I was once as you are. I had feet but they walked in forbidden paths. I had hands and they handled unclean things. I had eyes but they saw nothing of God aright. But now my eyes see, my ears hear, and my hands handle the Word of Life."

Because she understood temptation was a constant threat to the celibacy of her people, Mother Ann devised modes of "lodging together" aimed at building a new kind of relationship between men and women based on twin pillars: equality of the sexes and separation of the sexes. She clearly perceived the long and painful battle women were going to have to fight before they would ever gain independence for their minds and bodies. She was determined to help free them.

Upgrading the position of women was of paramount importance to Mother Ann in her total rejection of marriage. For countless generations the supremacy of men had been accepted as Biblical truth, inspired by God. Mother Ann was one of the very few spiritual leaders to repudiate this time-honored hoax that goes all the way back to Adam and Eve. (Even so strong a religious reformer as Martin Luther could say smugly, "Women were created with large hips so they can stay home and sit on them.")

Starting with Mother Ann's powerful example, equality of the sexes permeated the Shaker history. Women frequently conducted worship or spoke at meetings and their voices were as influential as the men's. Undergirding all these revolutionary departures was Mother Ann's belief, so central to Shaker religion, in the duality of God. God was the "Eternal Two" who encompassed both fatherhood and motherhood at once.

"In the Shaker Community," wrote Shakeress Aurelia Mace, "woman has taken her place as an equal with man, by intellectual if not by physical strength. Where there is an Elder, there is also an Elderess; where there is a Deacon, there is also a Deaconess, and they are considered equal in their powers of government." Incredibly, the Shakers achieved this at a time when a woman was never given employment equal to a man's. No wonder people were angered by Mother Ann's audacity.

The Shakers considered the separation of the sexes essential in promoting equality. The brethren and the sisters were never permitted to be together alone

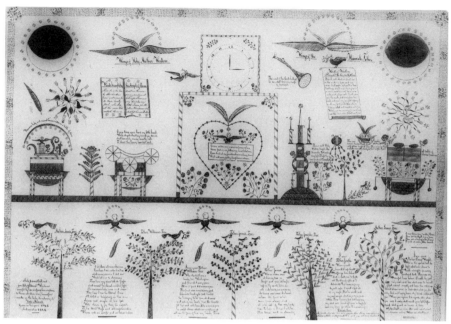

A sample of a spirit drawing which Shakers rendered as agents of the spirit. Some see these drawings as another way the Shakers sublimated the sexual urge. (Fruitlands Museums, Harvard, Massachusetts)

and all their living arrangements were completely separate. At meetings women entered through one door, men through another; the women sat on one side of the room, the men on the other. Touching of any kind was forbidden, even shaking hands.

Because Mother Ann felt that if men and women did not have some kind of informal relationship "they would surely have a carnal one," she originated "Union Meetings." Three times a week the brothers and sisters met together and sitting face to face, spent one hour "in friendly social intercourse with each other," talking or reading or singing.

Dancing, also part of "lodging together," was useful in sublimating sexual urges. Many people think of dancing as exciting sexual desire, but for the Shakers the opposite was true. During that strenuous part of their worship, the Believers gave vent physically to all their inner turmoil. In later years, as Shakerism developed, the dances became compulsory and exacting, but they remained invaluable safety valves that released the dancers from terrorizing anxieties.

There never was any touching. One observer described men and women "swiftly passing and repassing each other like clouds agitated by a mighty wind." Moving in square or circular formations they sang, clapped, and stamped, bowing and bending, often shaking their hands before them, as if to shake evil and sin out through the fingertips, or dancing with palms upturned, to symbolize the receiving of blessings. As the dancing grew ecstatic, the wild whirling caused some dancers to fall into a faint.

When pious neighbors protested against the blasphemy of combining worship with dance, Mother Ann was ready, as always, with a firm answer. "We take our authority from the Bible," she announced, reminding her critics that after David slew the giant Goliath, the Bible said: "David danced with all his might before the Ark of the Lord."

Mother Ann reinforced her followers with constant preaching and exhorting. "If you fight against the lust of the flesh," she told them, "you offer to God the first fruits of your lives. There is a glorious crown for all who struggle against the flesh in this world." In the place of sex, she urged tenderness, compassion, caring. She said Jesus called each person to be father, mother, brother, sister to everyone he or she encountered, and she called for the abandonment of sexual role-playing and even age roles. "We are not called to be one thing or the other — male or female, old or young," she said. "We are called to show forth the Divine — to be all things to all people."

After Mother Ann's death, nineteenth-century Shaker regulations for the total separation of the sexes became picayune. There were ridiculous prohibitions such as: *Brethren and sisters may not pass each other on the stairs. Sisters must not mend, nor set buttons, on brethren's clothes, while they have them on. Whispering is not permitted and blinking should never be practiced.*

The Shaker rejection of sex has always excited curiosity. Many people, repelled by the whole concept, have ridiculed their chastity vows. But the remarkable thing is that no case of scandal over sexual matters in any Shaker community has ever come to light.

Those who were angered by the peculiarities of Shaker life did not get close enough to discover that these people were trying to create a Utopian society ruled by the gentle law of love, where every hand was lifted for work and every heart bowed to God.

Mother Ann bore her neighbors' hostility philosophically. She knew it would be a long time before the United Society of Believers was accepted in rural New York. But she was not one to wait around for miracles; her way was to make them happen. Now was the time, she decided, to send out a missionary to tell the story of the Shaker faith and look for converts. She selected a dashing spokesman — her brother William Lee.

A tall, handsome man with long curly hair, Brother William had the magnetic Lee personality. Like his father, he had been a blacksmith in Manchester but he abandoned the family trade to join a royal cavalry regiment, the Oxford Blues. *Testimonies* describes William in England as "a proud, haughty young man, fond of gayety and able to dress himself in silks." It says he finally grew weary of high living and "fell into great trouble of mind because of his sins."

Sickened by guilt, William decided to consult his sister Ann about his problems. She was then leading a pious life in Manchester as a devout member of the Wardley Society. *Testimonies* continues: "When he arrived at his sister's being very gaily dressed, she reproved him for his pride, and convinced him of the wickedness of his life. He threw off his ruffles and silks and labored faithfully to find forgiveness for his sins and acceptance of God."

Mother Ann was far ahead of her time in comprehending the kind of power that is generated by guilt. She refused to accept the prevailing puritanical view that the proper treatment for guilt-feelings was self-inflicted punishment. Ann Lee knew from experience that guilt was an invaluable source of energy for change, a seed which could blossom into renewal of spirit. Her basic solution to the problem of guilt was simple: admit it in confession, then find atonement in work and worship. Brother William followed her instructions faithfully, and his whole way of living changed.

Converting her brother from playboy to penitent sinner is one more evidence of Mother Ann's forcefulness. Although he was only four years younger, William depended on her for guidance. She so awakened his conscience that he later said he felt his soul was "upon a needle's point" and he renounced his profession, home, family, and friends to join her crusade. Just as with the others, Mother Ann became William's north star. He said, "I love my Mother — although she is my Sister, yet she had become my Mother, and the Lord God has made me to love her."

Brother William Lee, "a man of sorrows, acquainted with grief," became the first itinerant Shaker minister in America — and a good one. Possessed of many talents, he was a fine singer, a skillful horseman, and an eloquent speaker. It was said he could do anything from laying out a garden in perfect order to drowning an accuser in a torrent of "bold language." Apparently he shared his sister's flaming gift for transmitting his feelings and his convictions to others, for Brother William brought many men and women into the Shaker faith.

One of his early converts was a woman with the apt name of Thankful Barce. In *Testimonies* she tells us what it was like to join the United Society of Believers:

> When I arrived, Mother Ann met me at the door, took hold of my hand and led me into the house. Her first salutation to me was in these words: "Being a daughter of Zion, how camest thou hither without a cap on thy head?" She sat down in a chair, and I sat down by her side. Her eyes were shut, and it appeared that her sense was withdrawn from the things of time. She sung very melodiously, and appeared very beautiful . . . The graceful motion of her hands, the beautiful appearance of her countenance, and the heavenly melody of her voice, made her seem like a glorious inhabitant of the heavenly world, singing praises to God. As I sat by the side of her, one of her hands,

while in motion, frequently touched my arm; and at every touch of her hand, I instantly felt the power of God run through my whole body.

Clearly, Mother Ann had a charismatic personality. *Charisma*, the Greek word for "divine gift," was originally used to describe miraculous powers the early Christians were said to possess, to heal, speak in tongues, and prophesy. Some of Mother Ann's disciples claimed similar gifts of grace for her; but she was careful not to presume Godlike powers for herself. To the people who came to her seeking forgiveness for their sins, *Testimonies* tells us Mother Ann would declare, "I can freely forgive you, and I pray God to forgive you. It is God that forgives you. I am but your fellow servant."

11

Ann Lee, "Spy"

Behold it is a time of war
And we have been enlisting,
Emmanuel we're fighting for,
And Satan we're resisting;
We have not in this war begun
To turn our backs as traitors,
But we will all unite as one
Against our carnal natures.

—Early Shaker Spiritual

ON MAY 10, 1780, — NEW ENGLAND'S FAMOUS "DARK day" — the sun never came out. Fearful souls were out wringing their hands and wailing, "The day of Judgement has come!" It happened that was the day Ann Lee had chosen for the first public testimony at Niskeyuna. No wonder the word went round that this woman possessed supernatural powers.

A Baptist minister named Issachar Bates gives a vivid account of that epic day in his autobiography.

There were neither clouds nor smoke in the atmosphere, yet the sun did not appear ... No work could be done in any houses without a candle! ... The darkness covered the whole of the land of

New England! And what next, right on the back
of this came on the Shakers! And that made it
darker yet . . . it was singing, dancing, shouting,
shaking, speaking with tongues, turning, preaching, prophesying, and warning the world to confess their sins and turn to God . . . All this was
right in the neighborhood where I lived.

The Shakers' behavior during the crisis impressed
Issachar Bates, for they turned to God while others
reacted by "cursing, blaspheming . . . and firing pis-
tols." Tempted to join the new movement, he added
somewhat wistfully, "But I was not ready yet, for I
had married a wife." Later Elder Bates brought his
wife and seven children into the faith and he helped
carry Shakerism into Kentucky and Ohio.

The public testimony attracted many people, for
under the leadership of Mother Ann and Brother
William, the Shakers were increasing in numbers.
But their enemies were also increasing. According to
A *Summary View*: "Such a remarkable event [the
conversion of large numbers to Shakerism] could
not take place without exciting great agitation in the
public mind. Hence many conjectures were in cir-
culation concerning these strange people, and
especially concerning their female leader. By some
she was strongly suspected of witchcraft, and the
old accusation was in substance revived: 'She casteth
out devils by Beelzebub.' "

With the spread of the American Revolution into upper New York, zealous patriots fanned the fires of suspicion that were already smoldering around the British-born folk at Niskeyuna. After the Yankees trounced the British at Saratoga, the Americans feared the English navy would retaliate by sailing up the Hudson and cutting the colonies in two. Albany, a strategic point of utmost importance, was gripped by hysteria and anyone with Loyalist leanings was considered dangerous. Rumors began to fly about that Niskeyuna was the hiding place for a network of British spies directed by a sinister woman who called herself "the Female Christ." Suddenly the Shakers were threatened with the kind of persecution they thought they had left behind in England.

The noted historian, Henry Steele Commager, says the most important thing in the American Constitution is freedom of religion; but this precious guarantee did not come easily. The struggle for religious freedom in America is a long and bitter story. Those who came to this country seeking "freedom of worship" did not always mean by the term a willingness to confer that right on others. Men and women with unorthodox convictions were hounded and abused in the New World as they had been in the old.

Anne Hutchinson was tried and ordered to leave the Massachusetts Bay Colony for preaching that true religion was found, not in a church, but in following God's guidance through the "Inner Light." Roger Williams, who refused to believe what the government told him to believe, was tried and banished from Massachusetts for his insistence that church and state must be separate. And Mary Dyer, a devout Quaker, was repeatedly arrested in Boston on the strange charge of "bearing witness to her faith." She was finally accused of sedition, condemned to death, and hanged in public.

Mother Ann is a less well-known but equally staunch figure in the procession of early Americans who were persecuted for their religious convictions. She had stipulated that the Shakers, like their Quaker colleagues, must be pacifists. As followers in Christ's footsteps, she said they could not aid or abet the sin of war and bloodshed. Mother Ann forbade them, absolutely, to fight anyone for any cause.

The burghers of Albany, preparing to battle the enemy on home ground, were not impressed by the Shakers' so-called "conscientious objection." "Arm yourselves only with meekness and patience," Mother Ann instructed her followers. The Believers, dedicated to the salvation of their souls, understood her words; but outsiders thought only a British spy would suggest such a thing.

"Tories!" cried the neighbors. They demanded that the Shakers swear their loyalty to America.

Testimonies gives us Mother Ann's reaction to that idea:

> General James Sullivan, with two other men of note, came to require the Elders to take the oath of allegiance to the country. The Elders refused to take the oath, and Mother Ann said to the General, "These men will never do you any hurt for they are well-wishers to the country. They will do all the good to the country that they are able to do."
>
> The General replied, "I want men to go and fight for the country."
>
> Mother answered, "You will never kill the devil with the sword."

It was impossible for the American patriots to understand that the Believers at Niskeyuna had no interest whatever in patriotism or in politics. To the Shakers, America was only one part of God's earth. It was the favored ground on which the kingdom of the Lord was first to be established, and they said of course they would cherish it, as they did all of God's universe. Fight for it they would not.

The more the Shakers tried to explain their position, the more they were considered suspect. When they began transporting extra food to Niskeyuna to feed their new converts, the patriots were sure they were supplying the British army with food and ammunition, while spying on the side. The festering boil of suspicion came to a head on a July day in 1780. David Darrow and Joseph Meacham were driving a flock of sheep along the road toward Niskeyuna when they were attacked by an angry mob. The two Shakers were captured and taken to Albany jail; the sheep were divided up among the crowd.

Mother Ann, Brother William, and James Whittaker were also arrested and thrown into the Albany prison. They were all accused of disloyalty to the American cause, but there is little doubt that the real objective was to get rid of these queer people who had been enticing solid citizens away from home, and church, and country.

Again the authorities demanded that the Shakers take an oath of allegiance. Again Mother Ann refused. She repeated that her people would have nothing whatever to do with the Revolutionary War. Some years later Mother Ann's pacifist convictions were codified in the Shakers' "Peace Document":

> Were mankind divested of pride and ambition, all wars would cease . . . We believe God has called us to this very work; and that it is required of us to set the example of peace and to maintain it at all hazards . . . We are firmly persuaded that those who subject themselves to the cross of Christ, and after his example, subdue the evil propensities which lead to war and strife, render more essen-

tial service to their country than they possibly could by bearing arms and aiding war.

The Shakers' arguments fell on deaf ears. Their leaders were charged with maintaining a secret correspondence with the enemy and publicly accused of treason.

Treason! What a dire word for peace-loving gentle folk to deal with! Back in England there had been two kinds of treason: high treason — the killing of a head of state; and petty treason — the killing of a husband by a wife or a master by a servant. (If the wife were killed by the husband, that was a much less serious crime.) High treason was marked off by a peculiarly ghastly punishment: public hanging, drawing and quartering.

In America, distinctions were not so clear-cut. Treason was defined as attempting to overthrow the government to which one owed allegiance. But which government was that? Most clergymen, for instance, still believed in the divine right of kings and, as members of the Anglican Church, prayed every day for the British king and his family. These ministers were not accused of treason, but then they were not, like the Shakers, asking people to reject the accepted values of society.

The jail in the Old Fort at Albany was a cold and forbidding spot; but Mother Ann, having spent so much time in prison in England, felt right at home there. She knew how to outwit confinement with her eloquent tongue and she attracted large crowds by preaching through the grates of her prison window. She told people that faith in God would carry them through any crisis and, thinking perhaps of her miraculous escape from death aboard the storm-tossed *Mariah,* added, "Faith is the anchor of the soul. It is like an anchor to a ship. When the winds blow and the waves run high, so, in like manner, faith will keep the soul steady in trials, temptations, and buffetings."

"Buffetings" is exactly what Mother Ann had to endure. To silence her, the Americans decided they would ship her to the British in New York City. Let the Tories cope with this woman who conversed with God in an English accent. Waging a revolution is difficult enough without having some woman, who attracts people like a magnet, repeating over and over: "No one who lives by wars and fighting can follow Christ."

The authorities placed the "Elect Lady," as they jeeringly called her, on a sloop headed for Manhattan. They hoped that was the last they would hear of her. Shakeress Mary Partington, at her own request, was allowed to go with her.

Mother Ann's boat got only as far as Poughkeepsie where once again she was jailed. *Testimonies* says:

During Mother Ann's confinement in Poughkeepsie jail, she was generally treated with kindness; and Mary, who was not considered as a
prisoner, had full liberty to procure necessaries
for her at the groceries. But for most of the time,
she was under great sufferings of soul; being deeply
impressed with the importance of the work before her, and feeling that her infant spiritual children had great need of her presence and protection, her soul was in continual cries to God.

Mary Hocknell, who had been left at the
Niskeyuna settlement, came down to Poughkeepsie
to try to help Mother. She stayed with one James
Boyd and his wife Nancy and, predictably, the Boyds
soon confessed their sins and "embraced the testimony." James Boyd must have been a man of influence because he managed to get Mother Ann
removed from jail and confined in his house.

At the Boyds, Mother Ann, her two female companions, and her hosts, "often engaged in the worship of God, under great power and operations of
the spirit." *Testimonies* recounts the local reaction
to their strange services. The picture of the citizens
of Poughkeepsie trying to burn out people at prayer
is not pretty.

Their behavior began to excite opposition among
some of the lower class of people in the town of

Poughkeepsie . . . One night, in particular, a number of the baser sort, painted and habited after the manner of Indians, came and surrounded the house, while the people were in the worship of God, and attempted to throw papers of gunpowder, through the windows into the fire, but, failing in their attempt, and being discovered, and sharply reproved by Mother Ann and James Boyd, they withdrew.

The attempt was secretly renewed some time in the night, and a large paper of powder thrown in at the top of the chimney, but fortunately, it bounded from the hearth, and did not take fire.

Following that public uproar, Mother Ann was sent back to the Poughkeepsie jail. Meanwhile, the Elders were suffering similar indignities at the Albany prison. One of them, the Reverend Samuel Johnson, was declared insane after his brother pleaded for his release on the grounds that he was out of his mind, "being formerly devoted to the cause of his country and zealous to defend her liberties by force of arms." The Reverend Mr. Johnson was discharged to his brother who promised to see he left the state; David Darrow was also paroled, because of his wife's illness, when his well-to-do father-in-law, Captain Jarvis Mudge, interceded for him; and eventually the others were released without formal trial of any kind. All except Mother Ann.

Oddly enough, imprisonment favored rather than hindered the Shakers. Some people objected to their mistreatment because it smacked of the kind of tyranny they had come to America to escape. Even in the midst of Revolution there were those who dared to speak out for civil liberty when they saw a defenseless group denied it.

The Shakers' prime objective was to free Mother Ann. She had been jailed in August and it was now December. The Elders knew the whole future of the United Society of Believers depended on the liberation of their leader. They ferried across the Hudson, hired a carriage and drove seventy miles over icy roads to Poughkeepsie to demand her release. To their dismay, the local constabulary flatly refused to discharge "the grand actress," as they called her. They still claimed she was a dangerous spy in the pay of the British.

The Elders did everything they could think of to get her out, but with no success. There was, finally, only one thing left to try: an appeal to the governor. It was decided Elder James Whittaker should call upon Governor George Clinton, who was then residing in Poughkeepsie.

George Clinton, "The Father of New York State," enjoyed great popularity. He was elected Governor of New York seven times and Vice-President of the United States twice, once with Thomas Jefferson and once with James Madison. At the time Elder James went to see him, Clinton was forty-one years old and had been governor only three years. He was a handsome, somewhat plump, man-of-the-people whose election had been a jolt to the establishment. (When he was made Governor of New York, John Jay wrote: "Clinton's family and connections do not entitle him to so distinguished a pre-eminence.")

Governor Clinton was known for "frankness and amiability in private life," but he must have seemed intimidating to Elder James Whittaker. A former military man, the governor was intensely patriotic and could be unmerciful toward Tories. Surely the gentle, devout Shaker approached him with trepidation. *Testimonies* says of that encounter:

> Elder James informed the Governor of their imprisonment, and related the pretense of accusation, and the manner of their treatment and sufferings. The Governor said it was the first knowledge he had received of the matter; and that he did not know there was such a woman in prison. Elder James, on his knees besought the Governor's assistance.

The sight of Elder James kneeling before him apparently moved George Clinton. He said he certainly was not in sympathy with jailing people for their religious beliefs. "In view of the length of incarceration," the Governor declared, "and due to lack of any treasonable evidence, aside from her refusals of oath, I believe the woman should be freed." It is interesting to note that twenty years later Governor Clinton visited the Shakers in New Lebanon and expressed pride in having "released their spiritual Mother from durance vile."

James Whittaker was required to post a two-hundred-pound bond for Mother Ann's "good behavior." This he was able to do with help from William Lee. They promised that she would not "say or consent to any Matters or Things inconsistent with the Peace and safety of this the United States," and then Mother Ann was released.

With great rejoicing the Brethren took Mother Ann and her companions, Mary Partington and Mary Hocknell, back to Niskeyuna. It was then the last of December, 1780. *Testimonies* says Mother Ann "was joyfully received by all her faithful children, in spiritual relation, after an absence of nearly five months. Thus ended the only imprisonment that ever Mother Ann suffered in America . . . By means of this event the sound of the Gospel trumpet, and the fame of 'Christ's Second Appearing' extended far and wide in this country." The happy Believers sang songs in praise of the rights of conscience such as:

> *Rights of conscience in these days,*
> *Now demand our solemn praise;*
> *Here we see what God has done,*

By his servant Washington,
Who with wisdom was endow'd
By an angel, through the cloud,
And led forth, in wisdom's plan,
To secure the rights of man.

The Shakers were the first organized group in America to speak out for conscientious objection to all wars. It was crystal clear to Mother Ann that their ultimate loyalty was not to man-made laws but to a peaceloving God. On this firm conviction she was willing to stand, like Milton's faithful seraph Abdiel, "unmoved, unshaken, unseduced, unterrified." It could be argued that Mother Ann Lee was more important to the nation than most of her famous contemporaries. For, in the words of Henry Steele Commager, "Those who think enough to be willing to sacrifice for conscience are the most valuable members of society."

12

Mother Ann's Enemies

"No one ever saved anybody, or served any
great cause, or left any enduring impress,
who was not willing to forget indignities,
bear no grudges. The world's saviors have
all, in one way or another, loved their
enemies and done them good."
—HARRY EMERSON FOSDICK

MOTHER ANN MIGHT BE DESCRIBED AS THE AVATAR OF
the Shaker movement. To the Hindus, who originated the word, an avatar was a God who appeared
on earth in bodily form. Mother Ann was not a God
to the Shakers but she was the embodiment of all
their religious beliefs.

The safe return of their "avatar," after her five
months in the foul prisons of Albany and Poughkeepsie, brought unbridled rejoicing to Niskeyuna.
Singing, dancing, and praying resounded far into
the night. Many were angry over Mother Ann's mistreatment but she told them reprovingly, "You can
never enter into the Kingdom of God with hardness
against anyone, for God is love, and if you love God
you will love one another."

Perhaps it was Mother Ann's obsession with the "completely other," the eternal, that most attracted people to her. For pious folk who felt a lack of substance within themselves, her intensity was hypnotic. They expected her to lift the whirling mists of daily life and let them perceive the shining world of the spirit.

Not surprisingly, a number of the converts who eagerly joined Mother Ann's crusade became sorely disappointed. They found their attempt at an entirely new life blocked by their own timidity, skepticism, shame, isolation, and fear. The experience of religious ecstasy, instead of freeing them from the iron grip of anxiety, only increased their tensions. Mother Ann's all-consuming passion for the absolute demanded too much. To reject everything worldly, even sexual love, was beyond them; and confession of all that lay buried deep within was impossible.

The Believers, who called the introduction into Shakerism "a time of sifting," were philosophical about those who "proved unworthy." The people who left the society fell into three groups: Winter Shakers, Bread-and-Butter Shakers, and Mortal Enemies.

The Winter Shakers enjoyed the comfort and warmth of the community during the cold months but when the robins sang in April, they departed. Mother Ann is quoted in *Testimonies* as telling some of them, "It is now spring of the year, and you have all had the privilege of being taught the way of God; and now you may all go home and be faithful with your hands. Every faithful man will go forth and put up his fences in season, and will plow his ground in season; and such a man may with confidence look for a blessing." A few did put up their fences and kept them repaired; the others fell into the old routines and let the disciplines of Niskeyuna fade from their minds.

Bread-and-Butter Shakers were nourished briefly by Mother Ann's spiritual diet, but they could not muster enough self-discipline to meet the stringent daily demands. This is illustrated by a laconic notation in an early Shaker record book: "John Short, Henry and George Grubb ran off to the world." The same book shows us how the Believers dealt with those who were unable to give up the fats and creams of everyday life: "Lucy Lemons was kindly invited to go to the world. She went."

The Mortal Enemies were the most difficult group to cope with. They were the men and women who left the society, for various reasons, and then hurled vitriolic attacks at the Shakers. One of the most vituperative was a Baptist minister from Stonington, Connecticut, named Valentine Rathbun. After Rathbun joined the society, he became infuriated because the Shakers refused to take oaths or bear arms in the Revolution. He departed in a rage, accusing them of being Un-American, Pro-British, Pro-Catholic (celibacy and confession being identified with Roman Catholicism), pagan, and immoral.

In 1785, the Reverend Mr. Rathbun published a pamphlet with the title: *Some Brief Hints of a Religious Scheme Taught and Propagated by a Number of Europeans Living in a Place Called Nisquenia, in the State of New York.* Since his booklet contains the earliest eyewitness account of a Shaker meeting, it is worth reading, bearing in mind that Valentine Rathbun's anti-Shaker, anti-British prejudice bordered on fanaticism. He reinforces his vivid indignation with lots of exclamation points.

To obtain instruction from the woman preacher, Ann Lee, I went to 'Nisquenia' and gave her a lengthy relation of my life. In return, she made me many wonderful promises . . .

Shakerism is a religion of bluff and its adherents are fanatics . . . I myself beheld the following, and know, therefore, whereof I speak . . . They meet together in the dead of night and have been heard two miles by people . . . They run about in the woods and elsewhere, hooting and tooting like owls . . . Very extraordinary but wicked movements in worship cause the Believers to gape, stretch, and twitch as though in convulsions. As these fits increase, so does faith in the Shaker

leader, Ann Lee. If onlookers try to bring worshippers out of these curious shakings and quiver-
ings, other worshippers cry out that the onlookers
will be damned for opposing the will of God.
Meanwhile, the victims are twitching and trembling as though afflicted by a terrible ague. Following this violence, sudden acute weakness sets
in and the worshippers fall helplessly to the floor . . .

Some Shakers sing songs. Some sing without
words in Indian dialects. Others sing jigs or tunes
of their own making which they call "new
tongues." While some dance, others jump up and
down — all this going on at the same time until
the different tunes, groaning, jumping, dancing,
the drumming, laughing, talking, fluttering, shov-
ing, and hissing, make such a bedlam as only the
insane can thrive upon. This Ann Lee calls the
worship of God! She speaks highly of her elders,
too, and says those men of hers are the Angels of
God sent to gather God's Elect! As for herself, she
has this to say: "I have the fullness of the God-
head bodily dwelling in me . . . Yea, Christ,
through me, is born the second time!"

Anybody opposing this blasphemy is threatened
with eternal damnation!

Most of those who join Ann Lee's movement
are urged to cry out against the military defense
of the country, against fighting the common British foe! All authority, I have heard her say — is
from Hell, and should rightfully go there again!

Ann Lee's scheming religion is not only treasonous, it is also aimed at breaking up life as we know it! She causes husbands and wives to part! She is responsible for the dissolving of society in peaceful neighborhoods!

Some of the women Shakers strip naked in the woods, thinking they are angels and invisible, and can go about among men and not be seen!

I am convinced the spirit which prevails over this new scheme is the spirit of witchcraft! . . . Ann Lee is Satan in the guise of a sweet angel of light . . . As the Devil himself at first deceived the woman and made use of her to delude the man, so is he playing once again his old prank by sending us this woman, Ann Lee . . .

In the midst of this country's great decay of religion and virtue, Ann Lee and her elders play their magic games . . . and try to bring the whole creation of man to trial. The scheme of that self-styled Female Christ, Ann Lee, is so naked that every rational mind should recoil at the thought of falling in with it! Yet multitudes have done so . . . And when people are so easily and erroneously carried away, it bespeaks their abysmal ignorance of the truth. MAY GOD PRESERVE YOU!

This tirade is signed "Valentine Rathbun, Minister of the Gospel, the public's REAL friend and humble servant!"

A quarter of a century later, Thomas Brown, one of the Shakers who also left the Society (he was said to "have got hold of the wrong chain"), wrote a book in 1812, *An Account of the People Called Shakers.* Brown said he asked the aged Mary Hocknell about the report that in Mother's day men and women danced naked together. Her answer was: "Because the brethren pulled off their coats, or outside garments, to labour, or as the world call it, dancing; and in warm weather the sisters being lightly clothed, they would report we danced naked. And you know how apt the ignorant and vulgar part of mankind, are to misrepresent what they see. If one told they danced part naked, or with but few clothes on, another in telling the story, would leave out the part, or few, and so it was reported, obviously, we danced naked."

Clearly Mother Ann was a controversial figure, as is anyone who takes a strong stand. Another violent attack, launched upon her by an unstable woman named Mary Marshall Dyer, made the Reverend Valentine Rathbun's words sound pale.

Mary and Joseph Dyer, with their three children, joined the United Society of Believers in 1811, twenty-seven years after Mother Ann's death. Mary became disillusioned with Shakerism after four years and left. She then sued the Shakers for taking away her husband, her children, and her property and devoted herself to writing lurid pamphlets about them. She charged that "the Shaker spirit is magnetism mingled with sexual passion." Her insistence that the Believers were obsessed by sex may have contained a grain of psychological truth. It could be argued that their fierce rejection of "carnal nature" indicated an intense preoccupation with it.

Much of Mary Marshall Dyer's venom was directed toward the Founder, Mother Ann. In a libelous onslaught called *The Rise and Progress of the Serpent from the Garden of Eden*, she accused Mother Ann of being a fortune-teller, a sadist, a prostitute, and a drunk. She quoted Mother Ann as saying, "Rum was the Spirit of God, and one of his good creatures," and added that the leader "made much use of it, as did her followers, but after Ann Lee's death drunkenness abated." Dyer's book, published in 1822, was printed and distributed at her own expense. Apparently no one else wanted to be connected with it.

The idea that alcohol played an important part in the early days of Shakerism seems totally incompatible with the rigorous discipline of the early Believers' lives. Some of the Shaker songs may have contributed to the accusation that Mother Ann was a drinker, although it seems apparent that the intoxicant referred to in verse is religious ecstasy, not liquor. One, for example, praises "Mother's wine."

Drink ye of Mother's wine,
Drink drink drink ye freely,
Drink ye of Mother's wine
It will make you limber.
If it makes you reel around,
If it makes you fall down
If it lays you on the floor
Rise and take a little more!

Both Valentine Rathbun and Mary Marshall Dyer hurt the Shakers' reputation. However, Mary indulged in such verbal overkill that she defeated her own purpose. She accused Mother Ann of having little children stripped naked and whipped, strung up by their wrists, left alone all night in the woods, and sometimes beaten to death. Even people who disliked the Shakers refused to believe Mother Ann would ever abuse a child. Mary Marshall Dyer lost her lawsuit against the Society and it was recorded officially that she had tried to "cast a stigma on the Shakers which they did not deserve."

Perhaps at the bottom of the angry attacks by Shaker enemies lay cold, clammy fear. Since the Believers were convinced they were in touch with supernatural powers, their peculiar worship, their singing and dancing and visions, may have frightened people. Many were superstitious in those days when the whole world was filled with unexplained happenings. Why would the sun suddenly be eclipsed? Why did countless women die in childbirth? Why would lightning burn up a tree? Why did an entire community suddenly succumb to illness? Who knew the answers? That unpredictable doubt-free woman living in the forest and communing with spirits must have seemed threatening. As Martin Luther said in an earlier, but equally superstitious time: "Many demons are in woods, in waters, in wildernesses, and in dark, pooly places."

The obvious answer to the bitter attacks by Shaker enemies is the indisputable fact that Mother Ann attracted to her new religion many men and women of the highest character and intelligence. She taught them, and embodied in her own life, precepts of honesty, hard work, cleanliness, and thrift that are totally incompatible with the kind of excesses of which she was accused.

No matter what accusations were made against Mother Ann, she always refused to reply in kind. "Keep a strict watch over the words you speak," she told her followers, "that you may not treat others unkindly nor cast on them unpleasant reflections. Let your words be few and seasoned with grace."

She insisted that Shakerism should be judged by its achievements, and she stood on the Biblical precept, "By their fruits ye shall know them." Through all vicissitudes she stressed the power of love. "God is love, and if you love God, you will love one another." One of the Shaker hymns tells us how her people responded to her lead:

> *Love, love, is a blessing*
> *It is worth possessing —*
> *Mother's love is precious and pure,*
> *So I will labor for love, love, love,*
> *Mother's love will always endure.*

13

The Ghost of Shadrack Ireland

Learn not to be the masters but the
mothers of the souls entrusted to
your care.
—SAINT BERNARD OF CLAIRVAUX (1090–1154)
A founder of the Cistercian Order

"YOU MUST NOT LOSE ONE MINUTE OF TIME,"
Mother Ann told her disciples, "for you have none
to spare." When she decided, in the spring of 1781,
to travel through the northeast to spread the Shaker
faith, it was true that *she* had little time to spare.
Though just forty-five, she had only three years of
life left.

Mother Ann considered it urgent to take Shakerism "to the world" because she believed the survival
unit for mankind is the whole human race. She spoke
of the "corporate nature of becoming" and said there
could be no such thing as individual salvation because "we are all members one of another."

Accompanied by five of her disciples, Mother Ann

set out from Niskeyuna in May to journey through Massachusetts and Connecticut proclaiming the testimony. With her were her brother, now called Father William, Elder James Whittaker, Samuel Fitch, Margaret Leland, and the ever-faithful Mary Partington. They were to be gone two years on what *Testimonies* called "a triumphal tour and a march to the cross."

Just before leaving, Mother Ann turned to Margaret Leland and said, in her typically colorful but cryptic language, "Margaret, you have come to fall upon the Rock, but if the Rock should fall upon you, it would grind you to powder."

The six missionaries, eager to share "the gifts of God" with the world's people, stopped first at Tucconock Mountain in the Berkshires. During their ten-day visit — again according to *Testimonies* — "Great power of God, with much manifestation of the power of the spirit upon the physical body, attended the testimony, as was usual where ever Mother Ann ministered; this was also followed by much opposition. One Doctor Hollebert attempted to dispute with the Elders, but being confounded and put to the blush by Elder James Whittaker, he went and advised the mob to let them alone; so no acts of violence were committed."

This pattern was to be repeated many times during Mother Ann's New England journey. As the

Shaker missionaries went from town to town their religious fervor aroused enthusiasm among many of their listeners but bitter antagonism among others. And the Shakers did not always find a Doctor Hollebert to turn away the angry crowds that pursued them.

By now Mother Ann had a wide reputation. Men and women, old and young, came by the hundreds to hear her and to quiz her. Life was tense and uncertain for people who lived on the frontier and they were captivated by Mother Ann's unwavering conviction that she had found God. She seemed to entertain no doubts whatsoever. Tirelessly she preached the life of self-denial — rejection of the world and the flesh, confession of sin, and pursuit of the Spirit in private prayer and communal worship. "Labor to make the way of God your own," she told them. "Let it be your inheritance, your treasure, your occupation, your daily calling. Labor to God for your own soul as though there was no other creature on earth."

Despite the war, Mother Ann talked to people about non-resistance, about loving their enemies. She often quoted the Book of Proverbs: "A soft answer turneth away wrath"; and she had ample opportunity to prove her point. A *Summary View* says:

> Every evil report and every wicked device . . . were called forth to calumniate and debase the character of Mother Ann and her companions, and render

them odious in the eyes of the people . . . The charges of being enemies and traitors to the country; of having fire arms and munitions of war concealed among them; of living in drunkenness and debauchery, and practicing witchcraft and other base crimes, were continually alledged against them.

The Shakers not only met hostility with soft answers, they tried music as well. They would undoubtedly have agreed with William Congreve, the English dramatist who wrote: "Music hath charms to soothe the savage breast, to soften rocks, or bend a knotted oak." The universal language of music was to them one of God's most magical gifts. They sang wherever they went — songs of greetings and songs of farewell, ritual songs, "gift" songs, dance songs, hymns, and anthems. They taught many of their songs to the people they visited. Being unable to write music, the Believers developed their own system of notation, using the first seven letters of the alphabet instead of notes.

As they rode along the dusty roads of New England, they improvised simple songs such as:

Oh, the gospel of Mother
What blessing it brings
Of substance not obtained
In earthly things.

Mother Ann loved the singing. Once she leaned from her carriage and called to the men following on horseback, "Brethren, be comfortable! Brethren, be joyful!"

"We will, Mother," they answered. And *Testimonies* adds: "Singing joyfully, they arrived at David Green's."

They sang even when they were mistreated. While James Whittaker was being beaten by a mob in Shirley, Massachusetts, *Testimonies* says, "Elder James had a new song of praise put into his mouth." In the midst of vicious persecution, Father William Lee composed a wordless tune that became famous among Shakers as "Father William's Dove Song." His voice was "melodious and powerful" and his songs were described by the Believers as "seeming like music from some superior being."

In his book about the Shakers, Thomas Brown was scornful of Father William because he was always seeking "to praise the Lord with dance and song." And, judging by Brown, Father William had difficulty giving Mother Ann's "soft answer." Once while he was preaching, a youth in the crowd made fun of him.

Lee took him by the throat and shook him, saying, "When I was in England, I was sergeant in the King's lifeguard, and could then use my fists;

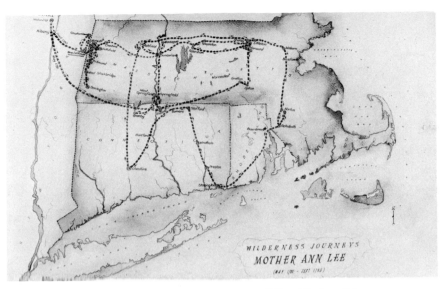

A map of Mother Ann's journeys. (The Shaker Museum, Old Chatham, New York. Photographer Lees Studio)

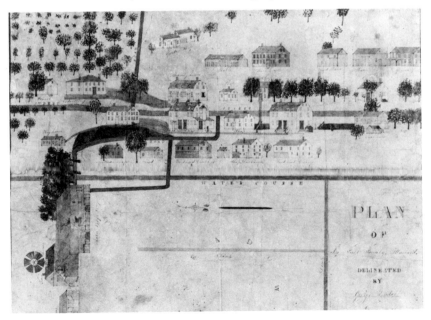

A drawing showing the Shaker settlement in Harvard, Massachusetts. The Square House appears as the larger of the two houses in the upper left. (Fruitlands Museums, Harvard, Massachusetts)

but now, since I have received the gospel, I must patiently bear all abuse, and suffer my shins to be kicked by every little boy. But I will have you know that the power of God will defend our cause."

The Shaker missionaries reached Harvard, Massachusetts, at the end of June, 1781. Mother Ann liked the peaceful village above the Nashua River, with Mount Wachusett in the distance. As soon as she saw the Square House at the end of town, surrounded by green meadows and dark pine forests, she announced this was the place she had seen in her visions in England and they were going to stay there.

Clara Endicott Sears's book, *Gleanings from Old Shaker Journals*, tells the story of how the Shakers managed to move themselves into the Square House.

> Father William spoke to Abigail Cooper, who was living in the Square House with Abigail Lougee. "Are you willing we should come into your house?"
>
> "No, I don't know as I am," Abigail Cooper replied.
>
> (Previous to this Abigail had gotten a little hint they were going to try to get in at the Square House to make their home there. Knowing they were English people, her feelings were not favorable to them.)

"Well, you'll let us come in, will you?"

"I suppose I must."

They came in and after taking their seats, Mother Ann said, "All we want is to help souls to God."

"I have seen a great deal of false religion," replied Abigail, "and I don't want to see anymore. If you have a new religion you can keep it to yourselves, for all of me."

Mother Ann, looking at Abigail, said, "I have seen you before." Looking around at the rest, she said, "I have seen all of you before."

Mother Ann asked Abigail if she loved them and Abigail said she did not. Then Father William handed Abigail an apple and said, "We will make you love us before we leave the place."

Abigail later said, "I did not want the apple but I took it. Before long I could say in truth I did love them. I loved the apple they gave me, for their sakes. When I was about my work I would look at the apple, and take it in my hand. I knew there was something good about them because I loved them, and I was thankful to take them in, and glad to do anything for them that I could do."

Abigail Lougee's home was called the Square House because of its unusual square roof. It was a roomy, well-built place, just right for big meetings. (The original house is gone now but the stone steps, the huge maples, and the stone walls remain.) The house had formerly belonged to an eccentric Baptist preacher named Shadrack Ireland, who died just before the Shakers arrived.

Once a disciple of George Whitefield, Ireland was a religious fanatic who had quite a following of his own. Like the Shakers, he believed in celibacy — with a difference. He left his wife and children in Charlestown and moved into the Square House with his "spiritual bride," Abigail Lougee. His hidden life with his soulmate must have made Ireland uneasy because he built a cupola on the roof, with a trap door and hidden staircase to the cellar, and spent hours up there watching to see if anyone might be coming.

Unlike the Shakers, Shadrack Ireland believed, literally, in physical life after death. He told his followers *if* he died at all, he would certainly come back on the third day. When he did die, Abigail Lougee refused to have him buried. She and her friend Abigail Cooper expected Shadrack to return to life. They spent days and nights waiting eagerly beside his body, but he remained cold and stark. At last they could stand it no longer. Abigail Lougee had the Reverend Ireland placed in a coffin and had the coffin bricked up in the Square House cellar.

According to records kept by the Harvard Shakers, Mother Ann had not lived in the house long before she was awakened in the middle of the night by a spine-chilling visitation. She got up, woke everyone in the house, and called a meeting. "We must all pray for the power of God," she said, "for there are the darkest spirits here that I ever sensed. Shadrack Ireland is *here*. He began in the spirit and ended in the most total darkness of the flesh."

Mother and all her people went "into the labors, or danced" to dispell Shadrack's sinister spirit. No ghost could be a match for Mother's zeal, and Shadrack Ireland's spirit must surely have been exorcised from the Square House that night.

The early records show that the Shakers bought the Square House; that Mother Ann contributed $144.17 toward the purchase; and that Mother Ann personally converted Shadrack's "spiritual wife," Abigail Lougee, to Shakerism.

Mother was able to persuade Abigail Lougee that the body was not immortal. "The evidence of the senses," she told her, "makes the claim ridiculous." She also lectured Ireland's followers on the subject.

> You are old people now, all of you, and you think you shall never die. Look at yourselves! You carry about you all the marks of mortality, just as other people do. Your skins are wrinkled; your hair turns white and is falling; your eyesight is failing; you are losing your teeth and your bodies are growing feeble. How inconsistent to think you shall never die. All natural bodies must die and

turn to dust! *Repent,* for the Kingdom of God is at hand!

Soon the Square House was the center of a whirling vortex of religious enthusiasts seeking salvation. Hundreds of men and women came there to be converted and to learn Shaker worship. Mother Ann said worship is changing the set of a person's mind, and this she knew how to do. Her exhortations brought forth joyous shouts and mournful wailings that were heard all over town.

"Love that power!" cried Mother Ann, as the "gift of shaking" seized the converts, "for it is the shaking of the dry bones, to bring bone to its bone." Even people who were not sure what she meant were affected by Mother's vibrations. It is not surprising that a woman whose motto was "Do all the good you can, in all the ways you can, as often as you can, to all the people you can" would attract others. All kinds of people came to Mother Ann for help. One woman tottered in weeping because her swollen legs were so painful. Mother Ann, who had the power to reduce anxiety, placed her hands upon her and the woman's legs were cured. No wonder she said of Mother Ann, "Her smile was like sunshine."

Many others spoke of Mother Ann's infectious smile and laugh. She enjoyed a joke, and she was utterly without pretense. When a visitor complimented her on her extraordinary humility, she replied, "I always admired pride — in a horse." But Mother's humor was kindly. A Shaker maxim that has been handed down from the early days, may have originated with her: "Jests and jokes are edged tools, and very dangerous to use, as they wound the tender feelings of our friends."

Not everyone at Harvard appreciated Mother Ann's talents. One of her converts, a "spoiled girl" named Jemima Blanchard, first came to the Square House to confess she had been telling people Mother was a witch. Mother Ann took Jemima by the hand and said, "I forgive you, and pray God to forgive you. There is no witchcraft but sin."

Soon afterward Jemima Blanchard, entirely against her parents' wishes, "put away her sins and became a child of God." Young Jemima must have found Shakerism highly exhilarating because *Testimonies* says: "She would sometimes go from the Square House to the South House, whirling rapidly and passing over fences, or whatever came in her way, without touching them or making the least effort to clear them. At times she would be entirely supported by the power without touching any material thing."

While the Shakers were living in Harvard, a wild rumor began to spread that the world was coming to an end. Every generation seems to confront this fear at one time or another. Many people sought

Mother's help because they were terrified that "the end" was near. She had no time for such frenzy. Over and over she told them she was not concerned with the end of the world. "I am only concerned," Mother Ann said firmly, "with the end of *worldliness.*"

14

Is She Really A Woman?

Anatomy is destiny.
—SIGMUND FREUD

MANY CELIBATE SECTS AND ORDERS HAVE APPEARED throughout religious history, but the Shakers were the only ones who ever required chastity of males and females living in a closely knit community, including some who once had been husband and wife. This extraordinary life style ignited the wrath and indignation of people who refused to believe that men and women, working intimately together, could abstain from sexual contact of any kind.

Issachar Bates, in his autobiography, records some of the accusations that were leveled at the Believers, by "religious" leaders. "The very air and woods," wrote Bates, "rung with the appalling sound of False Prophets! Seducers! Deceivers! Liars! Wolves in sheep's clothing! Parting man and wife! Breaking up families and churches!" He describes the relish with which village gossips whispered rumors that the Shakers castrated their males, stripped and danced naked during their night meetings, and went on perverted debauches. It was even said that the babies born of their unlawful embraces were secretly murdered. Although Bates calls this vicious talk "the croaking of bullfrogs," it undoubtedly inflamed the smoldering prejudice against the Shakers.

Mother Ann was a lightning rod, attracting much of the violent anger. Whenever she exhorted, in her vivid language, against sexual lust and the sins of the flesh, she was insulted by hostile crowds. As one Shaker historian wrote: "The fact of a woman presuming to preach and teach against the natural life, against the good Bible command to 'multiply and replenish the earth' was cause for decisive action. No matter if the earth were already replenished to repletion, 'til actual starvation threatened themselves and their children with death, that command they would adhere to, no matter what others were broken."

"Decisive action" of the most deplorable kind is what Mother Ann was subjected to one bitter December night in Petersham. Soon after she established the Shakers in the Square House, she left Harvard to take the testimony of the Believers to the neighboring towns of Shirley, Littleton, Woburn, and Petersham. Word was spread around that Mother Ann was a "virago," a derogatory word for a woman who had "masculine qualities of mind and body." Some said she was not a woman at all; she was a man dressed up like a woman. Certainly she was unlike any woman ever seen in Petersham, Massachusetts. Several tough characters in the town decided to kidnap her so they could examine her and find out for sure if she were a male or a female. *Testimonies* tells the whole shameful story with careful attention to detail:

> This being the first visit that Mother Ann and the Elders made in Petersham the inhabitants generally manifested a desire to see and hear her for themselves, and as they pretended civility, they had full liberty.
> Accordingly, on Monday evening there came a considerable number of civil people, also a company of lewd fellows . . . who styled themselves the blackguard committee.
> Elder James Whittaker . . . then began to speak . . . the mob had opportunity to arrange themselves through the assembly without being much noticed. Instantly a cry was heard, "Knock out the lights!"
> The lights were all suddenly extinguished, except the one in Elder James's hand . . . At this

instant entered three ruffians painted black, and rushing forward, the foremost one seized hold of Mother, and, with the assistance of his comrades, attempted to drag her out, but Elizabeth Shattuck and several other sisters instantly clinched hold of her, and held her, and Elizabeth being a large, heavy woman, and the passage narrow, the ruffians were not able to accomplish their purpose; and quitting their hold they suddenly fled out of the house.

In this struggle . . . they tore a breadth out of a new gown which Mother had on. Their wicked design being now fully known, Elder James advised to have the remainder of the assembly withdraw . . . But Mother, in the spirit of prophecy, said the wicked would come again . . . However, as the mob had withdrawn and all danger apparently at an end, the neighboring Believers returned home . . .

Those who remained were about retiring to rest when Mother discovered from the window, that her cruel persecutors were near, and made some attempts to conceal herself. The house was again assaulted by about thirty creatures in human shape; the doors being fastened, were burst open and broke, and these ruffians entered . . .

Elder James Whittaker was clinched by the collar, knocked down and left for dead; and several others were knocked down. Father William Lee was also hurt, and all who stood in their way were beaten and bruised . . .

As their object was to seize Mother Ann, the candles had been previously concealed to prevent their finding her. But this did not hinder them; they seized fire brands, and searched the house, and at length, found her in a bedroom; they immediately seized her by the feet, and inhumanly dragged her, feet foremost, out of the house, and threw her into a sleigh with as little ceremony as they would the dead carcass of a beast, and drove off, committing, at the same time, acts of inhumanity and indecency which even savages would be ashamed of.

In the struggle with these inhuman wretches, she lost her cap and handkerchief, and otherwise had her clothes torn in a shameful manner. Their pretense was to find out whether she was a woman or not.

In this situation, in a cold winter's night, they drove nearly three miles to Samuel Peckham's tavern, near Petersham Meetinghouse. Father William Lee feeling great concern for Mother's safety, he and David Hammond followed the sleigh. He told the ruffians that she was his sister and he would follow her; and, attempting to hold on to the hind part of the sleigh, they gave him many blows with the butts of their sleigh whips . . .

It appeared that Samuel Peckham was a Captain of militia, and had previously agreed with the ruffians who seized Mother, to give them as much rum as they would drink, on condition that they would bring her to his house. After they arrived

Father William Lee and David Hammond remonstrated against the ungodliness and brutality of their behavior. David presented to them the unlawfulness of such conduct, and how they had exposed themselves to the penalties of the law.

Being by this time ashamed of their conduct, and fearful of the consequences, they promised to release Mother Ann upon condition that David would sign an obligation not to prosecute them for what they had done. Being impelled by a feeling for Mother's safety, he reluctantly yielded to their demands, and left them to answer at the bar of Divine justice . . .

This being done, they released Mother Ann, and some time in the night some of them brought her and those with her back to David Hammond's. She came in singing for joy that she was again restored to her children (meaning her spiritual followers). The men who brought her back appeared to be greatly ashamed of their wicked conduct, and confessed that they had abused her shamefully, said they were sorry for it, and desired her forgiveness. Mother Ann replied, "I can freely forgive you, I hold nothing against you, and I pray God to forgive you;" so they departed peaceably.

After their departure Mother related the shameful abuse that she had suffered from these merciless wretches, and said, "It really seemed as if my life must go from me, when they dragged me out of my room, and threw me into the sleigh . . . they . . .

even tore some of the hair out of my head. But I was treated kindly at the tavern where they carried me. The tavern-keeper's wife kindly nursed and helped me. One of the men that took me away gave me his handkerchief to wear on my head, and another gave me his surtout to wear home.

Elder James Whittaker, who had been prevented from following Mother by reason of the severe wound which he had received, informed her of his abuses. His face was greatly swollen, and his jaw very painful, and he was apprehensive that it was broken; but, said he, "I can pray for them," and kneeling down, he cried, "Father, forgive them, for they know not what they do."

Mother Ann's capacity to forgive those who tortured her seems superhuman. How could she say "I hold nothing against you" to louts who had violated her person? Years before, when the mob tried to stone her to death in England, she had been able to declare: "I felt myself completely surrounded by God's presence and my soul was filled with love." Clearly, Mother Ann possessed extraordinary power, derived perhaps from her obedience to the instructions Saint Paul gave the early Christians in Rome (Romans 12:19-21):

Dearly beloved, avenge not yourselves, but rather give place unto wrath: for it is written, Vengeance

147

Two views of the marker on the spot where the Shakers were beaten; note misspelling of whipped. (Fruitlands Museums, Harvard, Massachusetts)

is mine; I will repay, saith the Lord. Therefore if thine enemy hunger, feed him; if he thirst, give him drink: for in so doing thou shalt heap coals of fire on his head. Be not overcome of evil, but overcome evil with good.

It is easy to imagine that Mother Ann's praying for the hoodlums who had captured her and explored her anatomy did indeed "heap coals of fire" on their heads. A person who is able to forgive a grave injustice gains great power. Mother Ann often used this power-of-forgiveness to try to awaken wrong-doers to the Christ Spirit she believed was within them. Although it did not always work with her enemies, it had an enduring effect on her followers, and is reflected in many of the Shaker songs. A typical hymn says:

> *I love Mother,*
> *I love her power,*
> *I know it 'twill*
> *Help me in every trying hour,*
> *Help me to shake up,*
> *Help me to break up,*
> *Help me to shake up,*
> *Every bond and fetter.*

While Mother Ann was away from the town of Harvard on her missionary travels, the goings on at the Square House alarmed the townspeople. As in the witchcraft hysteria in Salem a century earlier, fear was followed by panic and destruction. The first indication of trouble came when a company of militia forced their way into the Shakers' house on the pretext of searching for "a large cache of arms intended for the British." They found nothing, of course, but the Brethren who tried to keep the soldiers out of the sisters' quarters were bruised and bloodied.

On a hot morning in August hideous violence erupted in Harvard. Before dawn a mob surrounded the Square House. Armed with horsewhips and clubs, they had come to drive the Shakers out of town. As the mob charged into the house, the Believers knelt to pray for God's protection, but they were dragged into the street, some by the throat, some by the hair.

Then the cruel march began. The Shakers were driven like cattle for ten miles, from Harvard to Lancaster, in a shocking display of brutality. Old people were beaten as they struggled to keep up. Men and women who prayed aloud were whipped across the face. For "a little diversion," the marchers stopped to torture James Shepard, the only one in the crowd who had come from England with Mother Ann.

As they stripped Father James to the waist, he turned to the other Believers and said, "Be of good cheer, Brethren and Sisters, for it is your Heavenly

Father's good pleasure to give you the kingdom." They watched helplessly while Father James was scourged until "his back was all in a gore of blood and the flesh bruised to a jelly." Some Believers tried to cover him with their bodies; they, too, were unmercifully horsewhipped. William Morey, "a zealous Believer who denounced the ruffians for abusing the defenseless," had his teeth knocked out. With blood streaming from his mouth, Morey shouted at the mob, trying to shame them into stopping — to no avail.

When the gruesome parade finally reached Lancaster, the "distant brethren" from Niskeyuna were banished with a warning never to show their faces in Harvard again. The Harvard Shakers were herded back over the same weary miles. On the leafy road beside the Pollard house, near the spot where Father James had been horsewhipped, a Harvard Shaker named Abijah Worster was tied to a sycamore tree and beaten on his bare back for "going about breaking up churches and families."

That historic sycamore tree is still standing, its cream-colored trunk gigantic and its heart-shaped leaves spread against the sky high above the many-windowed house of Thaddeus Pollard. A stone slab nearby bears the shameful inscription: "On this spot a Shaker was whipped by a mob for religious views in 1783."

At the end of that infamous day, Father James and the others were bleeding and weak, but uncowed. They sang songs of praise to God and gave thanks that they, like the heroes in the Bible, were deemed worthy of suffering persecution for their faith.

Why did the gentle Shakers incur murderous anger wherever they went? Perhaps others considered their way of life — so God-centered and loving, so disciplined and dedicated — a commentary on their own lives. Injury to a person's self-esteem often produces aggression. When normal human beings — filled with self-concern and greed — witnessed the Shakers' heroic attempts to reform the human spirit, fury was probably inevitable. As one early Shaker record expressed it: "Such genuine marks of Christianity were too much for the seed of Cain to endure."

Mobs continued to pursue Mother Ann and the Elders as they made their way back toward Niskeyuna. When they reached New Lebanon, they felt as if they were coming home; but soon after their arrival Mother Ann was dragged into court again. While Judge Eleazer Grant watched unconcerned, the constable attacked her with his staff. He gave her a severe blow across her breast, undoubtedly aimed at discovering whether or not she was a woman. *Testimonies* records that "she carried the mark of it for sometime afterward."

Turning to the judge, Mother Ann said, "It is your day now, but it will be mine, by and by. Eleazer Grant, I'll put you into a cockleshell yet."

After a bond had been posted, Judge Grant allowed Mother Ann to go free, but a mob prevented her from getting into her carriage. Grant's reaction gives us a picture of the prevailing attitude toward a female who dared to speak out in a male-dominated society. He came to the door and said, "As magistrate of the state of New York, I desire that there be no mobs, nor riots." Then he added slyly, "Lay your hands on *no man.*" *Testimonies* says: "These words he repeated several times, laying a peculiar emphasis on the last words, *no man.*"

The judge disappeared into the building and was seen no more that day. The mob took his words as a license "to abuse Mother at their pleasure, seeing she was a *woman.*" This they did until she was rescued by her followers.

Miraculously, Mother Ann survived all the tribulations and torments she encountered in her trip "to the world," but her suffering took a toll. Her robust health was broken. By the time the travelers reached the ferry opposite Albany, she was weak with fatigue and her extraordinary stamina was gone forever.

A number of Indians were at the ferry and when they saw Mother Ann drive up in her carriage, they cried out, "The Good Woman is come! The Good

Woman is come!" Having endured so much abuse, Mother must have been comforted by the warmth and friendliness of the Indians.

She and the Elders ferried across the broad Hudson and proceeded on until they entered the forest, northwest of Albany, where they made a little stop and rested themselves in peace. Some wanted to stay overnight, but Mother Ann was eager to return to the colony she loved so much. They journeyed on, finally arriving at Niskeyuna about eleven o'clock on the night of September 4, 1783.

They had been gone two years and four months, traveled hundreds of miles, and suffered indescribable hardship and persecution. Mother Ann had introduced Shaker worship in many communities and founded Shaker societies in six places: Niskeyuna and New Lebanon in New York; Enfield in Connecticut; Hancock, Harvard, Shirley, Tyringham in Massachusetts. She never got as far north as Maine and New Hampshire; the Shaker colonies that were to flourish there came after her death.

Mother Ann had started on her New England journey in the spring of 1781, during the darkest days of the American Revolution. She returned the day after the peace treaty was signed, concluding what America's friend, the English statesman William Pitt the Younger, called "a most accursed, wicked, barbarous, cruel, unnatural, unjust, and diabolical war."

Eight long, bitter years after a ragged volley was fired at Lexington Green, the war was over. America had won its independence.

The Shakers took no part in the Revolutionary War, nor would they ever take part in any war. Their record of complete pacifism is unblemished. During the eight bloody years of the Revolution they labored with single-minded zeal to establish in America the Society of United Believers in Christ's Second Appearing. When Lord Cornwallis surrendered to George Washington at Yorktown, the band played "The World Turned Upside Down." When Mother Ann was asked why Shaker values were so different from the world's values, she had replied, "We are the people who turned the world upside down." Each in his own way — American Shaker and American soldier — were part of the great unending drama of a free people attempting to establish a free nation.

15

La Fayette Visits Niskeyuna

Who will bow and bend like a willow,
Who will turn and twist and reel
In the gale of simple freedom,
From the bower of union flowing.

Who will drink the wine of power,
Dropping down like a shower
Pride and bondage all forgetting,
Mother's wine is freely working.

Oh ho! I will have it,
I will bow and bend to get it,
I'll be reeling, turning, twisting,
Shake out all the starch and stiff'ning!
                                    —Shaker "gift song"

THERE ARE TWO WAYS TO BE RICH. ONE IS TO HAVE A
lot of money; the other is to have very few needs. At
Niskeyuna, early in 1784, an interesting confrontation took place between these two poles-apart
points of view when the Marquis de La Fayette came
to call on Mother Ann Lee.

It would be hard to imagine two people more opposite in every way. La Fayette, the aristocrat, was
born to vast wealth. Mother Ann, child of the slums,
sprang from dire poverty. La Fayette was brought
up on the rich liturgy of Roman Catholicism. Mother

Ann, rejecting ritual, believed simplicity of life nourishes the soul. He dressed in lace and gold braid. She wore homespun and called for "plainness in all things." He owned chateaux, fine horses, works of art. She gave up all earthly possessions in order to consecrate her life to God. He had a Frenchman's palate for rich delicacies and rare wines. A *Summary View* says of Mother Ann: "When occasion required, she would cheerfully make her meal on the fragments left by others, and say, 'This is good enough for me, for it is the blessing of God, and must not be lost.'"

General La Fayette, the complete militarist, relished warfare. He wrote in one of his letters: "I love the profession of war passionately and believe myself born on purpose to play that game." Mother Ann, the complete pacifist, preached nonresistance to her people, quoting from the Sermon on the Mount (Matthew 5:44): "I say unto you Love your enemies, bless them that curse you, do good to them that hate you, and pray for them which despitefully use you, and persecute you."

La Fayette was passionately in love with his child bride whom he had married when he was sixteen and she was twelve. Mother Ann considered sexual passion the root of all evil and she never lost an opportunity to "cry down those fleshly lusts which war against the soul."

La Fayette was one of the most powerful men in

France, politically and financially. Mother Ann had no power. She refused to participate in anything political, even voting. Such things were "too worldly." The only power that interested her was the power of the spirit. A proud man, La Fayette was often accused of arrogance; she, inherently humble, chose the bowing and bending of the willow tree as the Shaker symbol of humility.

While Mother Ann was beset by enemies all her life, young La Fayette hardly knew what a personal enemy was. Benjamin Franklin, then the American envoy to France, wrote to La Fayette: "You mention my having enemies in America. You are luckier, for I think you have none here, nor anywhere."

Yet as La Fayette grew older, his popularity waned and he was exploited by his friends. Late in his life, he was described as "a prince surrounded by people who flatter and despoil him, his fine fortune dissipated by adventurers and spies." Whereas one of Mother Ann's followers, describing the adoring Believers who visited her shortly before her death, wrote, "All sat on the floor on a carpet of Mother's love, soft as velvet."

When Marie Joseph Paul Yves Roch Gilbert du Motier Marquis de La Fayette was born in 1757, Ann Lee was a twenty-one-year-old factory worker struggling to survive in the slums of Manchester. Nothing could have seemed more unlikely than that these two would one day meet in America, discover common interests and express mutual admiration.

A lifelong, flaming idealist, young La Fayette was thrilled by the American struggle for independence. Since he was only nineteen, he knew he needed assistance if he was to join in the Yankee Revolution.

He sought help from a family friend, a septuagenarian then working in Paris to raise money for the Americans, that foxy statesman Benjamin Franklin.

Armed with a letter from Franklin to Washington, La Fayette abandoned wife, family, and career to offer his services to the new nation. He said he would ask no pay, just the supreme honor of being "near the person of General Washington." When he finally met his hero at a Philadelphia dinner in 1777 he said he recognized the great man at once "by the majesty of his face and figure."

One of the many concerns Mother Ann and La Fayette shared was a passion for liberty. After George Washington and his troops defeated the British, Mother Ann — dedicated pacifist though she was — knelt in thanks to God. She knew all too well what oppression did to people. The earliest written manifesto of the Shakers (1808) defines the Millennium as a time when "all tyrannical and oppressive governments shall be overthrown and destroyed, and mankind enjoy just and equal rights in all matters, civil and religious." La Fayette expressed a similar sentiment, but with a Frenchman's precision of language: "I have always loved liberty," he said, "with the enthusiasm of a religious man, with the passion of a lover, and with the conviction of a geometrician."

We don't know the exact date when the Marquis de La Fayette visited Niskeyuna, but in 1784 the Continental Congress sent him to upstate New York to conduct a peace powwow with the Indians. La Fayette, who gave them bales of colored cloth and bright trinkets, wrote General Washington from Albany: "My influence with the Indians was found greater than I myself could expect. I was, therefore, desired to Speak — to Hearken to Answers."

At some juncture, General La Fayette left the endless rounds of peace pipe passing to call on the "Good Woman" living in the Shaker settlement nearby. It is easy to guess one reason the French count was eager to meet Mother Ann. Earlier that year in Paris he had attended séances led by a doctor from Vienna, Friedrich Mesmer, whose group treatments, bordering on hysteria, were strangely similar to the ecstatic Shaker worship.

Like Mother Ann, Dr. Mesmer was a true mystic and a highly controversial figure. His very original psychic experiments in "animal magnetism" — the power one gifted individual could exert on others — inspired the hope that miracles can happen. A pioneer in psychotherapy, he believed he had made a discovery in the art of healing, as indeed he had. While the medical profession denounced him as a fraud, Mesmer proved he could cure some of his "mesmerized" patients through the power of suggestion and he teetered on the brink of discovering hypnotism. La Fayette was fascinated by the man and by his experiments.

When the Marquis heard tales of a magnetic woman near Albany named Ann Lee, whose persuasive emotional power gave her a gift for psychic elevation or "possession," he was naturally drawn to visit her. She undoubtedly gave him a warm welcome to Niskeyuna for she often quoted the Biblical adage (Hebrews 13:2): "Be not forgetful to entertain strangers, for thereby some have entertained angels unawares."

What did they look like, these two? A picture of La Fayette in his twenties shows an aristocrat with a long, pointed nose, slightly protruding eyes, and full lips. His white wig is rolled into twin coils above his ears and tied back by a velvet ribbon. In his high collared uniform with a lace jabot he looks the height of elegance.

Regrettably, there is no picture of Mother Ann, but Peter Bishop of Montague testified that Mother was the most beautiful woman he ever saw. Many of her followers spoke of her "compelling blue eyes" and her "inner radiance." Obviously, much of her beauty came from within.

The Marquis spent an entire day at Niskeyuna. In her book, *The Shaker Adventure*, Marguerite Melcher says, "La Fayette sat quietly watching and listening to what was going on about him. His interest was roused by the strange manifestations of spiritual influence that he saw. He entered into conversations with Mother Ann, raising many questions about the Shaker faith."

Surely he must have been intrigued by a woman who could say, "You may let the moles and bats have the gold beads, jewels, and silver buckles — that is, the children of this world — for they set their hearts upon such things; but the people of God do not want them . . ."

Unlike most men in the eighteenth century, La Fayette had no difficulty accepting a woman in a strong leadership role. He took great pride in his ancestor whose title was "Companion-in-Arms to Joan of Arc," and he respected the rights of women, as he did the rights of every human being.

On the surface it appears that the Marquis de La Fayette and Mother Ann were as unlike as mountain and stream; in fact, they had some strong similarities. Both were born leaders, blessed with warm, magnetic personalities and adored by their followers.

Both radiated sincerity, charm, goodness, and total dedication to their beliefs. Both possessed a childlike naïveté that led them into zealous idealism.

Both abhorred the scourge of the times — slavery. La Fayette wrote John Adams from Paris in 1786: "In the cause of my black brethren I . . . most assuredly side with them against the white part of mankind. Whatever be the complexion of the enslaver, it does not, in my opinion, alter the complexion of the crime which the enslaver commits, a crime much blacker than any African face." Mother Ann, revolted by slavery, accepted as final truth Jesus' statement (Matthew 25:40) : "Inasmuch as ye have done it unto the least of these my brethren, ye have done it unto me."

A contemporary describes La Fayette in words that could just as easily describe Mother Ann: "The Marquis de La Fayette possesses brilliant courage, remarkable serenity in danger, powers of discourse, popular manners, and rare elevation of soul." Another contemporary draws an even stronger parallel. Charles Sainte-Beuve wrote: "Had La Fayette lived in the Middle Ages, he would have founded, by the power of a fixed moral idea, some religious order."

At the end of La Fayette's visit to Niskeyuna, according to Melcher, he asked Mother Ann "why he himself might not become a sharer in this new way of life. Mother Ann told him that his time had not yet come to share in this spirit. She added that a great work and much suffering lay before him in this world before he could enter into the spiritual plane."

Fifty years later, when La Fayette died, in May, 1834, some of the Shakers claimed they received word of his death "by spirit messenger" days before the news was brought to America by boat. They recalled Mother Ann's prophecy of long ago. La Fayette had indeed known "much suffering." He had fought in the bloody French Revolution, lost his fortune, been declared a "traitor" by the French Assembly, and endured the misery of five years in an Austrian prison.

Mother Ann Lee and the Marquis de La Fayette were both reformers who dreamed the impossible dream. La Fayette — the liberal — saw what was wrong with society and tried to correct it. He fought for religious tolerance, emancipation of the slaves, trial by jury, freedom of the press, abolition of the nobility, and government by and for the people.

Mother Ann — the radical — saw what was wrong with society and *knew that all of its ills were connected*. She believed man's inhumanity to man could only be corrected by the advent of a new spiritual community. And she stood firm in her conviction that the tangled skeins of today are as nothing when measured against the endless tapestry of eternity.

16

The Death of Mother Ann

How much they are deceived,
Who think that Mother's dead!
She lives among her offspring,
Who just begin to spread;
And in her outward order,
There's one supplies her room,
And still the name of *Mother*,
Is like a sweet perfume.

—Early Shaker Spiritual

THE SHAKERS BELIEVED NOTHING EVER "RAN OUT OF use, an item or a person." As the days left to Mother Ann became fewer and fewer, she began to tell her children how to take care of things when she was gone. She laid great stress on their stewardship of God's earth, especially on cultivating the land "to yield her increase and develop her beauty." This must be done, she told them, in a spirit of love because "the earth yields most to those who love it." The Believers did as Mother directed, bestowing on the gardens and fields of "Wisdom's Valley" the attention that others bestow on family and worldly goods.

Having known privation in Manchester, Mother

Ann was appalled by the selfishness she had seen in America. "You must be prudent and saving of every good thing that God blesses you with," she said, "so that you may have wherewith to give them that stand in need. You cannot make a spear of grass nor a kernel of grain grow, if you know you must die for the want of it. It is by the blessing of God that these things come: therefore you ought not to waste the least thing."

Mother Ann never recovered her health after the turbulent trip through New England. Her once strong body grew increasingly weaker and she knew her hours were numbered. *Testimonies* says, "Mother sat in a chair almost all day and sang in unknown tongues, the whole time, and seemed to be wholly divested of any attention to material things." We can imagine her rocking and singing in her primitive rocking chair, now at Fruitlands Museum in Harvard, Massachusetts. A seven-rung Windsor chair with wide rockers fastened onto the legs, it was a crude forerunner of the exquisitely simple chairs for which later Shakers became famous.

As news of Mother's failing health spread, many came to visit her at Niskeyuna. She advised all who came of the importance of work-as-worship. Labor was sacred. She had told her disciple Calvin Harlow: "Before you become a great preacher of The Word, you will first have to get out and learn how to do

Mother Ann's Chair. (Fruitlands Museums, Harvard, Massachusetts)

manual labor." And she told her visitors: "When you return home you must be diligent with your hands, for godliness does not lead to idleness. The Devil tempts others, but an idle person tempts the Devil. When you are at work, doing your duty as a gift to God, the Devil can have no power over you, because there is no room for temptation."

Hand in hand with hard work, on Mother Ann's list of priorities, was cleanliness. "Good spirits do not live where there is dirt," she said. "There *is* no dirt in heaven." One young woman who came was amazed by the cleanliness, order, and simplicity she found at the Shaker settlement. She said, "Though I was brought up in New England among good farmers, I never saw such neatness and economy as was here displayed in the wilderness."

Order in all things was Mother Ann's credo. She thought order "the creator of beauty and the protection of souls." But the order she cared most about was interior order. "You must first establish order within yourself," she said. The true source of unhappiness, she believed, was the incoherence in people's lives caused by barrenness and confusion within.

Saint Augustine said he was a question to himself. For the dying Ann Lee there were no questions. Years before, she had tackled the immense, seemingly impossible, task of self-reconstruction. This she had achieved with invincible fortitude by cutting away all her personal desires in order to reach God. Her singleness of purpose seemed to fulfill the Biblical prophecy that "when the eye is single, the whole body is full of light." Now she was able to face her own death with equanimity. She had confronted the dark tides within herself and was in touch with the deepest part of her being where there were pools of harmony and peace.

For some time Mother Ann had felt premonitions of death. When planning for the future she would say, "You may live to see it, but I shall not." She forecast the opening of Shaker communities as far west as Ohio and Kentucky where "there will be a great work of God"; and Shakerism did flourish in those states for nearly a hundred years.

Often she spoke of her approaching death in parables. Like Jesus, she knew that story telling is the best way to teach. *Testimonies* tells of her gazing at an apple tree in full bloom and saying to Shakeress Hannah Kendall: "How beautiful this tree is now! But some of the apples will soon fall off; some will hold on longer. Some will hold on till they are full half grown, and then fall off, and some will get ripe. So it is with souls who set out in the way of God. Many will set out very fair, and soon fall away; some will go further, and then fall off; some will go further still, and then fall; and some will go through."

One of the Sisters, Eunice Goodrich, who was apparently not given to understatement, said, "So great was the manifestation of the power of God in Mother Ann at this time that many were unable to abide in her presence. Her words were like flames of fire, and her voice like peals of thunder, and her countenance beautiful and glorious."

While she was able to contemplate her own death calmly, Mother Ann found it excruciating to watch the deterioration of her younger brother, once so handsome and strong. In England William Lee had been skilled in "pugilistic arts" and after he joined the Shakers his ability to do hard work was legendary. Once he shoed a horse at a smithy in Harvard, then asked the owner of the shop what he owed. "Nothing," the man replied. "If a man can work like that, it is pay enough to watch him." Now at the age of forty-four, William Lee was feeble and afflicted. On a summer's day, he asked one of the brothers to sing to him, and while he was listening to the music Father William "passed into the world of the spirit." The date was July 21, 1784.

Father William was the first of the original English group to die. The cause of his death is not clear. *Testimonies* says, "He did not appear to die by any natural infirmity; but seemed to give up his life in sufferings." Mother Ann was sure he died as a result of the violence he encountered on their travels, and he did take to the grave wounds he received defending her. Many years later, when his bones were moved to the Shaker cemetery at Watervliet to rest beside his sister, it was discovered that his skull had been fractured.

After Father William's death, Mother Ann's grasp on life grew more tenuous. Although she firmly believed he was enjoying a better life, she was desolate without him. Her feelings are reflected in the Shaker hymn:

> *I know how to pray,*
> *I know how to be thankful,*
> *For God has blessed me*
> *With a broken heart.*

From then on she "continually grew weaker in body," *Testimonies* states, "without any visible appearance of bodily disease." By September it was apparent that the end was near. Job Bishop, who later founded the Shaker colony in New Hampshire, recalled talking with her three days before her death. "I shall soon be taken out of this body," she told him. "But the Gospel will never be taken away from you, if you are faithful. Be not discouraged nor cast down; for God will not leave his people without a leader."

Death "had no dominion" over Mother Ann, for in that ecstatic moment when she had the vision in Manchester jail, she surrendered herself completely and unconditionally to God. She lived the rest of her life "on a wonderful threshold."

Always relating the immediate to the infinite, she had told her followers, "Live together, every day, as though it was the last you had to live in this world."

When her last days came, her words were faithfully recorded by the Believers.

To John Barns she said, "You think that you will yet subdue and overcome the nations of the earth, but you are mistaken. They will have that work to do for themselves. They will fight and devour, and dash each other to pieces until they become so humble as to be willing to receive the Gospel."

To Anna Matthewson and Lucy Wright she said, "I see the opening of the heavens, and I see heavens of heavens, as it were, glory beyond glory; and still see that which does excel in glory."

Just before she died she murmured, "I see brother William coming in a glorious chariot to take me home."

"And when the breath left her body," *Testimonies* adds, "Elder John Hocknell, who was greatly gifted in visions, testified that . . . he saw a golden chariot drawn by four white horses, which received and wafted her soul out of sight."

She was only forty-eight when she died, but she had once said years before, "It is not important how long one has been in the work. What is important is how much work has been done."

Mother Ann's obituary, which appeared in the *Albany Gazette*, September 9, 1784, read: "Departed this life, at Nisquenia, Sept. 7, Mrs. Lee, known by the appellation of the *Elect Lady* or *Mother of Zion*, and head of that people called Shakers. Her funeral is to be attended this day." News of her death was carried by messenger to all Shaker "families" and many people, Believers and unbelievers alike, traveled out to Niskeyuna to attend her service.

Shaker funerals did not call for grief. The happy transference of the soul from the body into "a fusion of earthly spheres" was a time of inspiration. Instead of a formal ritual, Mother Ann's followers took turns exhorting others to follow her example. They said Mother could not die and was not dead and had not ceased to live among her people. She had only withdrawn from the common sight. She had cast off the dress of flesh and was clothed in a glory that concealed her from the world. She, Ann, The Word, the female embodiment of Christ, was transported to a realm where "there is neither bond nor free, there is neither male nor female, for all are one in Christ."

Father James Whittaker, to whom Mother Ann had passed the lead from her deathbed, said the union Mother Ann had experienced with Christ had given her extraordinary power to draw others to her. He

173

said if the Believers, like Mother, would cease to cling to the world and the flesh, they too could find that Truth which transforms life. "Be not conformed to this world," he cried, "but be ye transformed by the perfect will of God!"

Then they all sang spirituals overflowing with Mother's conviction that the Second Coming is here and now — a miraculous awakening within the heart and mind of each individual. Songs, perhaps, like this Prayer Song which sums up the life of Mother Ann Lee:

> *I never did believe*
> *That I ever could be saved*
> *Without giving up*
> *All to God.*
> *So I freely give the whole,*
> *My body and my soul,*
> *To the Lord God,*
> *Amen.*

Two brethren had dug her grave and two others had made her a wooden coffin "devoid of decoration." Lovingly, they placed it on a wagon and took her to the Shaker cemetery. There, near a flowing stream, they buried Mother Ann in a grove of maples and pines. Her plain marble tombstone reads:

174

A *rubbing of Mother Ann's gravestone. (Fruitlands Museums, Harvard, Massachusetts)*

ANN THE WORD

Mother
ANN LEE
BORN IN MANCHESTER
ENGLAND
FEB. 29, 1736
DIED IN WATERVLIET, N.Y.
SEPT. 8, 1784

Epilogue

Shakerism After Mother Ann

People who venture beyond common
concepts — such as the fear of
death — and come into the world
of the spirit are the true heroes.
—JOSEPH CAMPBELL

WHAT OF SHAKERISM AFTER MOTHER ANN'S DEATH?
Mother Ann's spiritual crusade might easily have
died with her. Father James Whittaker, who was
only thirty-three when he assumed the lead at her
death, died two years later. Luckily, Mother Ann had
converted two other strong leaders who were able
to take over. One was Joseph Meacham, called by
Mother her Saint Peter, "the rock upon whom the
church was founded." The other was Lucy Wright,
of whom Mother said when she first saw her, "We
must have that young woman. She will be worth a
whole nation." (Lucy's husband, Elizur Goodrich,
also became a Believer but, like Mother Ann, Lucy
preferred to keep her own name.) Both Joseph

Meacham and Lucy Wright were to prove more than equal to Mother's high expectations.

Elder James and Mother Lucy guided and goaded the Society with energy and skill and it expanded rapidly, first into New England and then westward. Eventually nineteen Shaker communities were established — two in Maine, three in New York, four in Massachusetts, four in New Hampshire, four in Ohio, two in Kentucky, and a small one in Indiana. At the peak of membership, just before the Civil War, there were six thousand Shakers who held in common ownership over one hundred thousand acres of land.

All the Shaker communities were beehives of activity. Although the Believers shunned materialism, they were so hard working and thrifty that almost without trying they became financially successful. (Most of their profits went into the purchase of land.) Because they believed work was worship, they labored ceaselessly and strove for excellence in everything. "Who does his best does well" was their motto. They used only the best materials and the things they produced were flawless. They seemed to have a genius for doing even the simplest things better than anyone else, and soon the world was beating a path to their door.

It was the Shaker inventions that first attracted the "world's people." Since the Believers thought it was important not to *overwork*, and since all work had to be interspersed with periods of prayer, they marshaled their wit and wisdom to make labor-saving devices. Their inventions ranged from the momentous to the minuscule. They invented the flat broom, clothespin, washing machine, circular saw, automatic spring, turbine water wheel, threshing machine, tongue and groove machine (for matching boards), revolving oven (to bake sixty pies at once), apple parer, stove-cover lifter, bread cutter, herb presser, sleeve ironer, spindle bender, table swift (a reel for winding yarn that sold originally for fifty cents and is now a museum item), pea sheller, berry-basket maker, potato peeler, pill dryer, peanut sheller, and a static electricity generator. In all, they are credited with over forty inventions.

Shaker ingenuity was boundless. They were the first to dry seeds and sell them in packets; the first to fashion cut nails and metallic pens; the first to make a four-wheel dump wagon; the first to air-condition beehives (by vents); the first to make permanent-press, water-repellent fabric; the first to weave palm leaf bonnets on a loom; and the first to market a manual for gardeners and herb medicines for the ailing. Who but the Shakers would think of putting a rack for a shawl on the back of a rocker, or buttons for tilting on the bottom of chair legs, or insulators on irons to hold the heat?

Constance Rourke in *The Roots of American Culture* writes: "Shaker fairness in matters of trade became a by-word throughout New England and even their enemies acknowledged that they excelled in mechanical arts." They excelled, too, in the cultivation of herbs, fruits and flowers, and the raising of livestock. Ironically, it was these material successes that made the Shakers acceptable in the eyes of the world.

The people who came to the communes to trade were dazzled by Shaker cleanliness and order. No spots of dirt or dust were permitted because Mother Ann had said evil spirits live where there is dirt. The extreme neatness of the buildings, fields, gardens, outhouses, and barnyards was almost beyond belief. Outside, the firewood was cut and stacked in exact order and, inside, only bare essentials were left in sight. Even the chairs were suspended on wall pegs (upside down to keep dust off the seats) so the floors could be swept several times a day.

Professor Silliman of Yale, one of many scholars who visited the Shakers, said, "Such neatness and order is not seen anywhere on so large a scale, except in Holland, where it is a necessity. Here it is voluntary."

Working, not for gain, but with loving care because their labor brought them closer to God, the Shakers created a style in architecture, in furniture design, and in crafts, remarkable for its bare-bones simplicity. Their craftsmanship was governed by a reverence for the uncluttered based on their conviction that objects with the greatest usefulness possess the greatest beauty. Their exquisite sense of symmetry came from their desire to express "the eternal two" — the duality of the Deity. Always they aimed at the perfection demanded for eternity.

Shaker style, now so widely imitated and sought after, was much too stark for the elaborate Victorians. Charles Nordhoff, a journalist and sociologist who made a study of communistic societies in America, admired the Shakers but criticized the severity of their work. "It seeks only the useful," he complained, "and cares nothing for grace and beauty, and carefully avoids ornament."

Nordhoff asked one elder, if they built anew, would they aim at "some beauty of design?"

The elder replied, "No, the beautiful, as you call it, is absurd and abnormal. It has no business with us. The divine man has no right to waste money on what you call beauty in his house or his daily life, while there are people living in misery."

Taste changes, and today few people would deny that the Shakers left the world a legacy of beauty. Now museums and collectors vie with one another to obtain examples of Shaker craftsmanship.

There is one facet of Shaker creativity which seems to contradict the belief that anything decorative or fanciful is "contrary to order." That is their nineteenth-century inspirational drawings or "gifts." About fifty years after Mother Ann's death, the Believers were engulfed by a wave of mysticism and spiritualism. An Era of Manifestations, which began at Niskeyuna in 1837 and quickly spread to the other Shaker communities, was characterized by divine messages from the world of the spirit, some in pictures, some in fine script. These unique spirit drawings are important both as an expression of Shaker faith and as an original American folk art.

Symbols abound in the delicate spirit drawings. Apples represent love; pears are for faith; roses for chastity; chains for union and strength; colored balls for comfort, light, and love. Precious jewels and exotic flowers are used to suggest the wondrous "heavenly sphere." Not surprisingly, some of the most exquisite drawings are the "gifts" sent from beyond the grave by Mother Ann herself: Shaker spiritualism ended in the 1860s and many of the drawings were destroyed. Those that survive are highly prized by collectors.

The Shaker legacy lives on in many contemporary arts also. There are the sunstruck, angular paintings of Charles Sheeler; the musical masterpieces of Aaron Copland (his *Appalachian Spring* uses the haunting Shaker melody " 'Tis A Gift To Be Simple"); and the moving re-creation of Shaker dance by Martha Graham's company.

Doris Humphrey, choreographer of that brilliant ballet, wrote perceptively about Shaker style, and their life style as well: "Directness, meticulous structure, immaculate line devoid of superfluous ornament . . . [these appear in] the uncluttered rooms of their functional dwellings, in their fastidious dress, in the austerity and practicality of their lives. Yet within these calmly balanced lives dwelt also the passion of religious exaltation and the tension of sexual frustration."

The Shaker prohibition against sexual intercourse has, over the years, excited considerable curiosity. Since all Believers adhered to the rule of celibacy laid down by Mother Ann, how, it is asked, did the Society maintain its membership? The answer is, new members were obtained by conversion and recruiting and — in the case of children — by adoption. The Shakers took in and lovingly cared for, all unwanted children, whether they were orphaned, abandoned, or illegitimate. But these children did not become Shakers automatically; they had to make that decision after they became of age.

Responsibility for raising the adopted children was shared by the whole Society. They taught their charges the useful arts and they emphasized character-building. Classical learning was considered "mere lumber of the brain." All schooling was subject to the work to be done since help was needed and the Believers knew that children who are busy are kept away from temptation and trouble. Girls went to school in spring and summer and boys in winter. During the autumn, everyone worked in the fields and kitchens.

In caring for the children of others, the gentle Shakers were guided by Mother Ann's law of love. At a time when a popular motto for parents was "love well, whip well," they remembered Mother Ann's words:

> Little children are innocent, and they should never be brought out of it. If brought up in simplicity, they would receive good as easy as evil. Never speak to them in a passion; it will put devils into them.

The world often poked fun at the Shakers, particularly for sexual abstinence. It was said by the ridiculers that they must multiply by division, like the amoeba, or expand by internal combustion, like the steam engine. Artemus Ward, a humorist whose misspellings were considered hilarious in the nineteenth century, wrote:

> The Shakers is the strangest religious sex I ever met. Why this jumpin up and singin? This long-weskit bizniss, and this anty-matrimony idee? My

friends, you air neat and tidy. Your lands is flowin
with milk and honey. Your brooms is fine, and
your apple sass is honest. . . You air honest in your
dealins. You air quiet and don't distarb nobody.
For all this I givs you credit. But your religion is
small pertaters, I must say. You mope away your
lives here in single retchidness, and as you air all
by yourselves nothing ever conflicts with your
pecooler idees, except when Human Nater busts
out among you, as I understan she sumtimes do . . . .

The gals among you, sum of which air as slick
pieces of caliker as I ever sot eyes on, air sying to
place their heds agin weskits which kiver honest,
manly harts, while you old heds fool yerselves
with the idee that they air fulfillin their mishun
here, and air contented. Here you air, all pend up
by yerselves, talkin about the sins of a world you
don't know nothin of.

What motivated six thousand American men and
women to become Shakers? Many of them abandoned their wives or husbands, their children and
possessions, because they wanted "a closer walk with
God." Others came to escape the tensions of family
life. At one time the only respectable way to obtain
a divorce was to join the Shakers. Still others sought
the comfortable moral freedom that goes with a
totally demanding, utterly unquestioned, faith. And
some joined after they had been transported by the

ecstasy of Shaker worship and found truth in Mother Ann's words, "You must seek your true religion where your deep bliss is."

Many nineteenth-century women were attracted by the Believers' conviction that it takes *both* man and woman to complete the image of God. In the Shaker community women were always treated as equals. There were no sexual stereotypes; it was all right for women to be powerful and for men to be tender.

Mother Ann was one of the first women in America to possess power, and to talk about women's rights in a tough-minded way. She offered her sisters a new way of living and it is not inconceivable that Ann Lee was the American founder of women's liberation. Deploring the male's ruthless "gratification of the flesh," she called for a balance between male and female at a time when women were totally subject to male dominance.

Not surprisingly, the Shakers attracted many famous visitors. Some viewed them sympathetically, some did not. Ralph Waldo Emerson in his *Journals* speaks of the Shakers "drudging in the fields and shuffling in their Bruin dance," but he gives them credit for possessing wisdom. In *Moby Dick*, Melville describes the archangel Gabriel as coming from "the crazy society of Neskyena Shakers."

Nathaniel Hawthorne, in his short story, "The

Canterbury Pilgrim," denounces Shakerism as unnatural. Writing about a young couple who were
seeking to become Shakers, he said they were going
to a community "where all former ties of nature or
society would be sundered, and all old distinctions
levelled, and a cold and passionless security be sub-
stituted for mortal hope and fear, as in that other
refuge of the world's weary outcasts, the grave."

No one was harder on the Shakers than Charles
Dickens. In 1843 he visited the Shaker community
at Mount Lebanon and said he felt about as much
sympathy for the brethren "as if they had been so
many figureheads of ships."

We walked into a grim room, where several grim
hats were hanging on grim pegs, and the time was
grimly told by a grim clock, which uttered every
tick with a kind of struggle, as if it broke the grim
silence reluctantly, and under protest. Ranged
against the wall were six or eight stiff high-backed
chairs, and they partook so strongly of the general
grimness, that one would much rather have sat on
the floor than incurred the smallest obligation to
any of them. Presently, there strode into this
apartment, a grim old Shaker, with eyes as hard
and dull, and cold, as the great round metal buttons on his coat and waistcoat; a sort of calm gob-
lin . . .

In the building where the Shaker manufactures

were sold the stock was presided over by something alive in a russet case, which the elder said was a woman; and which I suppose *was* a woman, though I should not have suspected it.

Dickens also noted, "There is no union of the sexes: and every Shaker, male and female, is devoted to a life of celibacy." He added that if all Shaker women resembled the one he saw, any deviation from that rule would be a "wild improbability." After a brief visit, he departed "with a hearty dislike of the old Shakers, and a hearty pity for the young ones: tempered by the strong probability of their running away as they grow older and wiser, which they not uncommonly do."

To counterbalance Dickens, we have the enthusiastic praise of Charles Lane, a wealthy member of the failed Brook Farm experiment who, after visiting the Shakers, wrote to Mrs. Bronson Alcott: "I think nowhere is the twofold purpose of human life, of being good and doing good, so fully provided for."

The peak of Shaker prosperity and influence was reached in the mid–nineteenth century under the dynamic leadership of Elder Frederick Evans. Contrary to earlier times when the Believers kept to themselves, Evans reached out to make many contacts with the outside world.

The Shaker dedication to pacifism attracted the

interest of Count Leo Tolstoy in Russia. He wrote from Yasnaya Polyana, to Elder Evans at Mount Lebanon, to enquire about the Shakers' attitude toward war. "I think," wrote Tolstoy, "the principle of non-resistance is the chief trait of true Christianity and the greatest difficulty in our times is to be true to it."

Shakerism is synonymous with peace, but Mother Ann's leadership in the peace movement has gone largely unrecognized. She and her devout followers were the *first* in this country to speak out for conscientious objection to all wars, and to refuse, under any terms, "to support the cause of war and bloodshed."

During the Civil War, when some of the Believers were drafted for military service, Elder Frederick Evans petitioned President Lincoln to exempt the whole sect from fighting, on the grounds of conscience. After listening to the argument, Evans later recalled, Lincoln leaned back in his chair and asked:

"Well, what am I to do?"
"It is not for me," Elder Frederick replied, "to advise the President of the United States."
"You ought to be made to fight," Lincoln said.
"We need regiments of just such men as you."

Nevertheless, Abraham Lincoln granted the Shakers' petition and the draftees were given an indefinite furlough.

Doris Grumbach, in a *Commonweal* article called "American Peaceniks," states: "The Shakers' most notable contribution to the life of this nation was, to my mind, their early impregnable pacifism and resolute conscientious objection."

The whole Shaker movement was a protest against the existing constitution of society. Emerson saw it as an important social experiment. He wrote in his *Journals* that the Shakers "were really the pioneers of modern socialism" whose example proved "not merely that successful communism is subjectively possible, but that this nation is free enough to let it grow."

The Shakers themselves, living day by day with the adage "Give all you have and take only as you need," believed they had introduced a new era of socialism, the age of the Millennial Church. But as the historian Henri Desroche says, "It was only a dream which was later to be filed away in the company of other 'Utopias' that have fallen victim to the harsh facts of reality."

It is sad when a noble dream dies. For two hundred years the Shakers *lived* righteousness instead of just talking about it. Now twilight has almost completely descended on that band of valiant idealists. Slowly the United Society of Believers in Christ's Second Appearing dwindled away. In 1909 there were a thousand members; by 1930 only a hundred; by 1950, a handful. Only two Shaker villages are left: one in Canterbury, New Hampshire, with three sisters, and one in Sabbathday Lake, Maine, with nine sisters. A third village at Hancock, Massachusetts, has lovingly re-created the Shaker way of life in a kind of museum. The last Shaker brother died in 1961 and since then no other men have been accepted because there is now no Shaker man to hear confessions, and women are not allowed to hear a man's confession. (Years ago the Shakers abandoned public confession in favor of private confessions, called "opening of the mind," which may take years to complete.)

Mother Ann foresaw the eventual decline of the Millennial Church. She said, "There will come a time when there won't be enough Believers to bury their own dead. When only five are left, then there will be a revival."

That time may be approaching. Today, interest in Shakerism has progressed from curiosity about their mores; to concern about preserving their crafts, music, and architecture; to admiration and emulation of their "gift to be simple."

The Catholic mystic Thomas Merton wrote of the vanishing Shakers: "After their departure these innocent people, who had once been so maligned, came to be regretted, loved and idealized. Too late people . . . recognized the extraordinary importance of the spiritual phenomenon that had blossomed out in their midst . . . The Shakers remain as witnesses to the fact that only humility keeps a man in communion with truth, and first of all with his own inner-truth. This one must know without knowing it, as they did."

The youngest living Shaker, Sister Frances Carr, forty-eight, says simply, "We'll go away in time, as will everybody. But our ideas and our way of life will never go away."

And so Mother Ann's dream lives on.

Author's Note

THIS BOOK WOULD NEVER HAVE SEEN THE LIGHT OF day had it not been for the gently needling, sometimes prodding, always supportive interest of my husband Tom Campion. If he hadn't dangled a trip to British Columbia before my eyes, I'd still be happily nestled in the library doing Shaker research. Two others who helped me beyond measure are Kitty and Russell Alspach, editors *par excellence*, whose belief in this book meant everything to me. The fact that these two brilliant scholars were able to slide down from the rarified atmosphere surrounding their variorum edition of W.B. Yeats to the N.R. Campion level was giddy encouragement.

Other editors, supporters, and gentle critics to whom I am indebted are our daughter Cissa

Campion, my brother Colonel Red Reeder ("King of the Literary Frontier"), and his wife Dorothea Darrah Reeder ("The Duchess of Accuracy"), my lawyer-editor-mentor Toby Dakin, and five perceptive encouragers: Betty Beckwith, Kathy Gardner, Alexandra Marshall, Roz Stanton, and Chris Hewat. I would also like to thank Ruth Hammen, precisionist; Dan Hodermarsky, builder-upper of the fainthearted; Gartha Allen, Thomas Merton enthusiast; Professor Winfred E.A. Bernhard, master researcher; and Dr. Henry Steele Commager, walking reference library.

I am indebted to the Robert Frost Library at Amherst College, and the William A. Neilson Library at Smith College, for their remarkably lenient booklending policies, designed to help, not hinder, aspiring writers.

Dr. Judy Speidel and Dr. Patrick Sullivan, of the University of Massachusetts School of Education, shared with me research done for "The Shaker Legacy," their slide-tape presentation. Thanks, also, to Marilyn Marlowe at Curtis, Brown, and John Keller at Little, Brown — pillars of patience. And to Jeanne Harlow and Janet Murdock, two young women who seem to enjoy reading the books they type, which can mean a lot to the author.

This book owes its origin to Sis and Andy Fisher of Nassau, New York. They were the ones who took me by the hand and introduced me to the wonderful world of Mother Ann. I'll not forget that blustery winter day at the Darrow School when they started me out on my Shaker journey. My gratitude to the Fishers is unlimited.

Three Shaker authorities have had an unwitting influence on this book: Amy Bess Miller, the woman whose foresight and energy saved the Hancock Shaker Community from extinction; Dr. William L. Lassiter, fabulous collector and author of *Shaker Architecture*; and Dr. Theodore E. Johnson, resident scholar and sage at the Sabbathday Lake Shaker Community in Maine, who conducted a brilliant three-day seminar to commemorate the 200th anniversary of Mother Ann's arrival in America. The three days I spent at that Sabbathday Lake seminar changed not only my book, but my life.

Warm appreciation also goes to the literary ladies of Nondescript Club in Bronxville, New York, and the Tuesday Club in Amherst, beautiful sounding boards.

NARDI REEDER CAMPION
Amherst, Massachusetts
January 6, 1976

Bibliography

Adams, Charles C. *The Community Industry of the Shakers.*
Albany, N.Y.: State University of New York, 1932.
Allen, Arthur B. *Eighteenth Century England.* London: Rock-
liff, 1958.
Andrews, Edward D. and Faith. *Shaker Furniture: The Craft-
manship of an American Communal Sect.* New Haven,
Conn.: Yale University Press, 1937.
————. *Visions of the Heavenly Sphere: A Study in Shaker
Religious Art.* Charlottesville: The University Press of Vir-
ginia, 1969.
Andrews, Edward D. *The Gift to Be Simple.* New York, N.Y.:
J.J. Augustin, 1940.
————. *The People Called Shakers: A Search for the Perfect
Society.* New York, N.Y.: Oxford University Press, 1953.
Axon, William E.A. "Biographical Notice of Ann Lee, A Man-
chester Prophetess and Founderess of the American Sect of
the Shakers." *Transactions of the Historic Society of Lan-
cashire and Cheshire.* Liverpool, England: 1875.
Bailey, Derrick S. *Sexual Relation in Christian Thought.* New
York, N.Y.: Harper and Bros., 1959.
Blinn, Elder Henry Clay. *The Life and Gospel Experience of
Mother Ann Lee.* East Canterbury, N.H.: Shakers, 1901.

Blumenthal, Walter Hart. *American Panorama: Pattern of the Past and Womanhood in Its Unfolding.* Worcester, Mass.: Achille J. St. Onge, 1962.

Brown, Thomas. *An Account of the People Called Shakers.* Troy, N.Y.: 1812.

Burr, Anna R. *Religious Confessions and Confessants.* Boston, Mass.: Houghton Mifflin Co., 1914.

Commager, Henry Steele. *The Search for a Usable Past.* New York, N.Y.: Knopf, 1967.

Cutten, George B. *The Psychological Phenomena of Christianity.* New York, N.Y.: Scribner's, 1908.

De Sanctis, Sante. *Religious Conversion.* New York, N.Y.: Harcourt, Brace and Co., 1927.

Desroche, Henri. *The American Shakers.* Amherst: University of Massachusetts Press, 1971. (Translated from French and edited by John K. Savacool.)

Dexter, Elizabeth Anthony. *Colonial Women of Affairs: Women in Business and the Professions in America Before 1776.* Boston, Mass.: Houghton Mifflin, Co. 1931.

Dingwall, Eric J. *The American Woman: A Historical Study.* London: G. Duckworth and Co., 1956.

Dyer, Mary Marshall. *A Portrait of Shakerism.* Concord, N.H.: 1822.

———. *The Rise and Progress of the Serpent from the Garden of Eden to the Present Day: With A DISCLOSURE OF SHAKERISM.* "Printed for the author." Concord, N.H.: 1847.

Evans, Frederick William. *Autobiography of a Shaker.* Albany, N.Y.: 1869.

Faxon, Alicia Craig. *Women and Jesus.* Philadelphia, Penn.: United Church Press, 1973.

Flexner, Eleanor. *Century of Struggle: The Woman's Rights Movement in the United States.* Cambridge, Mass.: Harvard University Press, 1966.

Gottschalk, Louis. *Lafayette and the Close of the American Revolution.* Chicago, Ill.: University of Chicago Press, 1942.

——— (ed.). *Letters of Lafayette to Washington 1777–1799.* New York, N.Y.: Privately printed, 1944.

Green, Calvin and Wells, Seth Y. *A Summary View of the Millennial Church of the United Society of Believers (Commonly called Shakers).* Albany, N.Y.: 1823.

Harkness, Georgia. *Women in Church and Society*. Nashville, Tenn.: Abington Press, 1972.

Hutton, Daniel M. *Old Shakertown and the Shakers*. Harrodsburg, Ky.: Harrodsburg Herald Press, 1936.

James, William. *The Varieties of Religious Experience*. London: Longmans, Green and Co., 1902.

Johnson, Paul E. *Psychology of Religion*. Nashville, Tenn.: Abington Press, 1960.

Ketchum, Richard M. (ed.). *The American Heritage History of the American Revolution*. New York, N.Y.: American Heritage Publishing Co., 1971.

Lamson, David R. *Two Years' Experience among the Shakers*. West Boylston, N.Y.: AMS Press, Inc., 1848. (Published by the author.)

Langdon-Davies, John. *A Short History of Women*. New York, N.Y.: Viking Press, 1927.

Lassiter, William Lawrence. *Shaker Architecture*. New York: Bonanza Books, 1966.

Mace, Aurelia G. *The Aletheia: Spirit of Truth*. Farmington, Me.: Knowlton and McLeary Co., 1907.

Melcher, Marguerite Fellows. *The Shaker Adventure*. Princeton, N.J.: Princeton University Press, 1941.

Neal, Julia. *By Their Fruits*. Chapel Hill, N.C.: University of North Carolina Press, 1947.

Nordhoff, Charles. *The Communistic Societies of the United States*. New York, N.Y.: Harper and Bros., 1875.

Oxley, William. *Modern Messiahs and Wonder Workers*. London: Trubner and Co., 1889.

Reeder, Colonel Red. *The Story of the American Revolution*. New York, N.Y.: Duell, Sloan and Pearce, 1959.

Rourke, Constance. *The Roots of American Culture*. New York, N.Y.: Harcourt, Brace and World, Inc., 1942.

Rudin, Josef. *Fanaticism: A Psychological Analysis*. Notre Dame, Ind.: Notre Dame Press, 1969.

Sanders, John. *Manchester*. London: Hart-Davis, 1967.

Sedgwick, Henry Dwight. *Lafayette*. Indianapolis, Ind.: Bobbs-Merrill Co., 1928.

Spaulding, E. Wilder. *New York in the Critical Period 1783–1789*. New York, N.Y.: Columbia University Press, 1932.

Symonds, John. *Thomas Brown and the Angels*. London: Hutchinson and Co., 1961.

BIBLIOGRAPHY

Testimonies of the Life, Character, Revelations and Doctrines of Mother Ann Lee, and the Elders with Her, through Whom the Word of Eternal Life was Opened in This Day of Christ's Second Appearing, Collected from Living Witnesses in Union with the Church. Edited by S. Y. Wells. Albany, N.Y.: 1827.

White, Anna and Taylor, Lelia. *Shakerism: Its Meaning and Message.* Columbus, Ohio: 1905.

Youngs, Benjamin Seth. *The Testimony of Christ's Second Appearing.* Lebanon, Ohio: 1808.

Index